Everything is an Event

Marinda Freeman
Everything is an Event

Copyright © 2024 Marinda Freeman
marinda@marindafreeman.com
(415) 203-6055

All rights reserved.

ISBN Paperback 979-8-9915548-0-0
ISBN ebook 979-8-9915548-1-7

Published by KWE Publishing, www.kwepub.com

Cover & interior design by Michelle Fairbanks, Fresh Design

Author photo by Stephanie Mohan of CreativePortraiture.com

First Edition. All rights reserved. No portion of this book may be reproduced, stored in a retrieval system, or transmitted in any form or by any means - including but not limited to electronic, mechanical, digital, photocopy, recording, scanning, blogging or other - except for brief quotations in critical reviews, blogs, or articles, without the prior written permission of the publisher, KWE Publishing.

Everything is an Event

A STEP-BY-STEP GUIDE

CREATING MEMORABLE OCCASIONS FOR TODAY'S LIFESTYLE WITH 15 PRINCIPLES REVEALED

Marinda Freeman

*Dedicated to my mother, grandmothers,
and many aunts—all accomplished hostesses,
amazing cooks, skilled seamstresses,
talented decorators, and artists from whom
I learned how to live my life.*

Table of Contents

INTRODUCTION 1

CHAPTER ONE: The Foundation Fundamentals—
Purpose, Atmosphere, Order, Flow... 11

CHAPTER TWO: The Essential Elements—Tools to Build Your Event 29

CHAPTER THREE: Mantras and Words to Live By... 43

CHAPTER FOUR: How to Plan and Use the Tools 61

CHAPTER FIVE: Tips and Tricks, Nuts and Bolts 87

CHAPTER SIX: It's Event Day..107

CHAPTER SEVEN: Virtual Events 133

CHAPTER EIGHT: In Conclusion 149

APPENDICES:

    Appendix A: The 15 Principles 153

    Appendix B: Event Timelines 154

        Summer Dinner Party Event Timeline
        (see page 107 for more about this event) 154

        Elaine & Lyman Wedding Weekend Event Timeline
        (see page 123 for more about this event) 155

        Big Sur Wedding Leni & Bryant Event Timeline 157

        Blank Excel Event Timeline 160

    Appendix C: Diagrams...161

        The Event Circle...161

        Blank Energy Bubble 162

    Appendix D: Prepping for Thanksgiving and any Holiday Meal 163

    Appendix E: Hors d'oeuvre Suggestions.. 168

Introduction

> *"Man is so made that when anything fires his soul, impossibilities vanish."*
>
> –Jean de La Fontaine

Everything is an event to me. It's a lifestyle choice to entertain whether at home or helping clients entertain their guests for a special occasion. That's how I think about a dinner party with a few friends, my daughter's birthday party, an anniversary celebration, or those bigger events, such as a gala fundraiser, a wedding, or any other special occasion. All these are opportunities to bring people together to connect, be in community, and have an enjoyable time—maybe even an inspiring time! It's also a way for me to show that I care for all those that attend, or to help my client show how much they care about everyone who is in attendance. I want guests to feel thrilled to be included, delighted to see old friends, meet new friends, and have a great time! Isn't that what every event is really about?!

When I was planning and managing events as executive director of Martha Stewart's catering business about four decades ago (where did the time go?!), I had already been coordinating events. It all came so naturally to me that it was difficult for me to communicate what I was doing. Yes, the successful results showed I knew what I was doing, and I developed many long-time clients because of this. When I meet with clients, many times, they don't know where to start even if they have a vision of the event they want to have.

If you haven't hosted an event for some time (the pandemic sure put a kibosh on all entertaining for a while), memory muscle may need to be revived. I wrote this book so you know where to start, how to think about your event from start to finish, and to have a great time doing so.

I think Thanksgiving dinner is an event, don't you? It starts with thinking ahead to the date and considering who you need to invite. Next step is calling or emailing, texting, or using another form of social media to invite your family and friends and confirm they will attend. Then you know how many you will have at your table. It's always a challenge to get everyone to respond. Don't hesitate to reach out again if you don't hear from them! It doesn't matter how many guests you have, it could be just a couple of close friends.

As the date gets closer, you order your turkey, plan your menu, make a shopping list, go shopping, and determine what needs to be made when. Pies and relishes can be made in advance, and the turkey and some of the other fixings need to be made the day of. The day before, you set the table so that it's not on the day-of list. Designing and setting a beautiful table lets everyone know that you care about them being there with you. All that planning, prepping, cooking, and then, it's time to sit down, enjoy the food, and connect with everyone around the table. Just reviewing this, are you exhausted and now don't want to prepare Thanksgiving dinner? Do you think the gathering of relatives and friends is worth it? I do.

Do you feel that the thought of planning a party of any kind puts you in a state of nerves and anxiety?

Or do you need to plan a special celebration or gathering and don't know where to begin?

Or do you feel overwhelmed with the task of planning a meeting or conference?

Or do you break out in a sweat just thinking about entertaining others?

This book is for you!

Perhaps, as an event professional, you find yourself challenged by clients who don't understand the work that you do.

Or does your boss not appreciate all the time and effort it takes to plan the events they want?

This book is for you, too!

You can also share this book with your clients (and boss) to clarify what it is you do.

This book will provide clarity and fifteen principles to follow to make your event planning successful. What I share will expand your understanding of how event planning principles work. Start with clarity of purpose and the intention to create community—the purpose of every event. And . . . I will be with you every step of the way! Planning ahead is the key to stress-free events.

There is no need to feel overwhelmed or stressed by the prospect of planning an important dinner party, a child's birthday party, a special celebration, a business gathering, or any event, for that matter. Having planned and produced all kinds of events from birthday parties and milestone celebrations to gala fundraisers, weddings, 5K walks, and more for forty years with my business, I will share with you the secrets I have learned to create events with ease and peace of mind for my clients—and, for my own home entertaining.

Sound impossible? Trust me, it's not. Really! You can do this! Follow the steps, the process, and the principles that underlie every event. Know these principles always operate with every event—and I have proved them over and over. I've also taught these principles to clients, nonprofit and corporate professionals, and even college students. Most of all, we want our guests to leave saying, "This was the best party (or event) I've ever been to!"

EVENT DESIGN—which is what I explain in this book—is thinking holistically about your event and how you want to express your lifestyle choices. Over the many years of designing events, I started to discover the principles of events. They are always operating whether you know them or not, just like gravity. We don't talk about the fundamentals, but they are always working. No one talked about these principles; however, as I started to clarify them and use them with large events I was producing, I witnessed them working and improving the **experience of the event for the guests**. I invite you to learn the fifteen event principles and follow the steps outlined in the following chapters, and you will be on your way to creating events with ease and joy . . . plus, the results will be rave reviews from your guests. *I am passionate about creating community, which is the point of every event. Bringing people together to connect*. At any event we attend, don't we want to feel at ease, delighted to be there, meeting new and old friends? You can create this experience for any event you plan.

I opened my event planning business in 1985, after managing Martha Stewart's catering company in Westport, CT, for two years, and then helping another friend double her catering business in a year and a half. I started my event business because I realized I liked putting all the pieces together. Event planning was not even a career back then. Now, they teach it in school. However, I don't think they teach what I have to share with you. Yes, you can make your planning and production of an event SO MUCH EASIER! And, more fun! My personal motto is *if you're not having fun, you're wasting time.*

I should probably back up and explain that prior to managing catering businesses, I taught private cooking classes in Manhattan for several years. Before that, I had a career in fashion, retailing and buying for stores in New York, San Francisco, and Tokyo. Before that? I was social chairman of my sorority for two years in college. Who knew that would be the start of a career down the line? Before that? In high school, I cooked dinner every night for my family (father, brother, and sister). I read and studied *Mastering the Art of French Cooking* and I also referred to *Joy of Cooking*. When I taught cooking classes, these were the two books I required that my students get. I've had a life-long passion for cooking, which started with baking at age five. When I lived in Tokyo for a year, I taught our translator how to bake, which is not something they did much in Japan. What I learned is that cooking has a language. To cook, you need to learn and understand the language. Separating two eggs does not mean one on the counter and the other in a bowl. Cooking is also about planning. There's an order you need to follow to make a dish or bake a cake. That means there's a recipe and a process to follow. It's the same with events. This book is your recipe for success!

I have organized this book in order of the steps to take to plan and produce your event. Here's a brief outline of what you will find in more detail in each chapter.

CHAPTER ONE:
The Foundation Fundamentals—Purpose, Atmosphere, Order, Flow

You can't build a house without pouring a foundation. The same applies to events. Before you start planning all the details, there is the planning before the planning. First and foremost is **clarity of purpose**. Why are you putting on this event? It is important to be clear about why you are planning the event and make sure everyone participating is on the same page. *You will keep coming back to the purpose over and over again as you start filling in the framework of your event.* The foundation also includes defining what the **atmosphere** will be and what the **experience** is that you want your guests to have when they arrive, during the event, and when they depart. This is based on your clear intention of what qualities you want your guests to experience. **How you think about your event will permeate every aspect of it.**

CHAPTER TWO:
The Essential Elements—Tools to Build Your Event

Having clarified your purpose and atmosphere, you are now ready to get organized. I call this creating order. Here you will find what tools you need to help you get and stay organized. This is the key to successful planning. Write lists, make spreadsheets, create a binder, have tabs in your binder for every aspect of the event, and have folders on your computer. Being organized also helps you think about the flow of the event from beginning to end. Creating timelines helps design and manage the flow of an event; plus, it's all written down, and you don't have to try to remember what and when everything is planned to occur.

Did you know that the attitude you have while planning your event is what will be expressed in the end result? For example, if you are planning a wedding, would you anticipate that everyone will have a wonderful, fun time where all connect with each other in celebration of the couple they know and love? Imagine that atmosphere as you put all the pieces together.

CHAPTER THREE:
Mantras and Words to Live By

As I tell my clients, focusing on the questions is especially important. Is everything in alignment with my purpose and goals? Do all the details support the reason for this event? Is there coherence? Do all the parts fit together to make an integrated whole? Am I continually looking at the macro—the big picture—and the micro—all the details? To help ask these questions, there are statements and words to live by. I call these mantras because I repeat them over and over—to remind myself of these truths and how to think about my planning and the actions required.

Everything is an Event

CHAPTER FOUR:
How to Plan and Use the Tools

Getting organized is the key to successful events. The more advanced planning, the more at ease you will be. This chapter outlines all the aspects of your event to consider, including how to write them all down and create a binder that holds all the information in one place. Since you are creating a physical event, you need a physical binder with all the information at your fingertips—not just online! The principle is—**order creates greater calm and peace of mind.** Years ago, I produced a large evening gala for a local nonprofit that had never had an event planner assist them with their annual event before. The setup day, the day before the gala, volunteers kept arriving. So many said to me, "It feels so calm! Nobody is running around like crazy." This is a reflection of advanced planning—which is more than they had had for previous galas.

There are tools you need for every event—a binder, a map, or layout if the event is a large one, and an event timeline—no matter what size the event is. The event timeline lists everything that occurs from setup, during the event, to breakdown. I will teach you to **Time Travel** using the event timeline to "do the event before the event." Something I do many times with clients prior to their events. You will want to do this, too!

CHAPTER FIVE:
Tips and Tricks, Nuts and Bolts

Sometimes, it's the little things that make a difference. Actually, most of the time, it's the little things and the not-so-little things that make a *huge* difference. Your guests may not notice them, but they would if you didn't take care of all those little details. This chapter explains many of the important aspects and nuts and bolts of planning an event.

All event details are addressed with one thing in mind—to TAKE CARE of the guests. After all the planning and before the event begins, I always tell my staff (or the volunteers) that the most important job they have is to TAKE CARE. Take care of the guests, the vendors, and anyone that is part of the event. Yes, the staff may have specific jobs to do at the event, but the overarching job is to take care of those in attendance. I'm sure you want your guests to feel appreciated and delighted to be there. I do.

CHAPTER SIX:
It's Event Day

You have spent the time to build a foundation by clarifying the purpose of your event, making sure that every aspect is in alignment with that purpose, and **Time Traveling** to "do the event before the event." Now, you have arrived on-site to set up, produce the event, and manage any breakdowns. Time to relax, have fun, and allow it all to unfold. You have already anticipated what might happen and taken care of every possible aspect. You are directing the action on-site like an orchestra conductor. If something shows up to be addressed, it is an opportunity for creative problem solving. In this chapter, I will show step by step what occurs during the event itself and how it unfolds.

After celebrating a successful event, get a massage. You deserve it! Also, remember that it's not over when it's over. There's always follow-up. With a large event, I write up an evaluation—what worked, what didn't work, what to improve—and review it with my client for planning next year's event. If it's a one-time celebration, there's always something to be learned for the next time you find yourself planning a festive occasion. There's always something that can be adjusted or tweaked to make an event better, even if it's just your next dinner party or child's birthday party.

CHAPTER SEVEN:
Virtual Events

We all have experienced a shift to virtual events with Zoom meetings and virtual conferences, or even virtual happy hours with friends. The planning and preparation remain the same. The principles and processes remain the same. The primary change is the venue, plus the technology that has changed to adapt to this new way of connecting. In this chapter, I outline my experiences producing virtual conferences, meetings, online tastings, as well as virtual celebrations of life. There are techniques to remember when you are producing a virtual event, and this chapter will explain them. This is a reminder that the principles work no matter what kind of event—in person or virtual!

CHAPTER EIGHT:
In Conclusion

As I say, it's never over when it's over . . . there's always follow-up. However, by following the steps in this book, the result will be a wonderful event, filled with memories and guests raving about what you created!

APPENDICES

The 15 Principles, Event Timelines, Diagrams, Tips and Menus

Before you start reading this book ...

{ Events may look like magic—I think they do, especially for the guests. They see the result, not the thinking, planning, and time that went into creating the end result. This book will lift the veil and share the magic of how to create events. It's fun, and when taken step by step, I know anyone can create a magical event. }

"To see a thing clearly in the mind makes it begin to take form."

–Henry Ford

Chapter One

The Foundation Fundamentals
Purpose, Atmosphere, Order, Flow

Whether planning a big or small event, you can learn how to use event principles. I have discovered fifteen principles that when followed guarantee you will have a successful event. Mostly, it's learning where to start when planning an event. I think everything is an event—from a child's birthday party or a dinner party to family holiday gatherings, weddings, anniversaries, bar mitzvahs, nonprofit galas, meetings, school functions, conferences, and large corporate events. The principles and practices remain the same. At a party or event, guests will talk about their experience. They will describe how the event made them feel—it was fun, I felt relaxed, it was comfortable, the space was beautiful, I met wonderful people, and so on. Do you wonder how to create that experience for your guests? You can do this. Just read on and follow the path I have outlined for you.

Planning and producing events are about holding the big picture of what you want to manifest. I call this **Event Design**. To design an event is to think holistically about it. This means knowing that the whole event results in an experience that is greater than the sum of its parts, although every part and every detail is important in building and supporting the end result.

PRINCIPLE #1:
CLARITY OF PURPOSE

The foundation for every event is to first clarify the **purpose** of the event. Make sure you and everyone else involved are clear about the purpose and all agree.

Why is clarity so important? If you start off on the wrong foot, you will be off track from the very beginning. It is essential to start with a clear purpose of your event. This is the foundation for all your planning. Refining and clarifying the purpose and your intention of the event is important so that everyone involved is clear about what direction you are going and why you are planning this event. With **purpose-driven events,** every aspect, idea, and action supports the purpose. All the details support the purpose.

PRINCIPLE #2:
EVERY EVENT IS AN EXPERIENCE

Once your purpose is clear and everyone is on board, then it is time to design the **atmosphere** that creates the **experience** you want your guests to have. Keep in mind these questions:

> **What do you want your guests to say when they arrive?**
> **What do you want them to say when they leave?**

Yes, you can design your event so that your guests speak your intention of what their experience will be. By designing the atmosphere your guests walk into, they will say what you intended them to say. Really! I've watched this happen many times. For a friend's holiday party, I came and helped rearrange the furniture to open the space. So many guests told my friend afterward that they loved getting to talk to everyone, which was the real purpose of her party. Nobody at my friend's holiday party said anything about how glad they were that the couch wasn't blocking the room.

PRINCIPLE #3:
CREATING CONNECTION AND COMMUNITY IS THE POINT OF ALL EVENTS

At a wedding, the bride and groom were clear that they wanted to have everyone feel connected. What did I hear the guests say as they were leaving? I felt like I was part of a big family, and I made so many new friends! Nobody talked about the location space, the arrangement of the tables, or the flowers. And the space was beautiful, which was a reflection of the intention for the guests to feel relaxed and connected.

When my daughter started elementary school, I was asked to help with the spring fundraising auction. I was told the purpose was to raise funds to supplement our children's elementary and middle school education. The first year I helped coordinate the auction, we used our local community center. Everyone had been in this space innumerable times. The auction event that year was called Rock the Boat. The committee chairs wanted to do something different—and also use boating as the theme. Draping the walls with pipe and drape in the entrance foyer removed all that was familiar on the walls and created a new look. Stepping inside the main room, there were four sailboats—or actually, four large sails hanging from the rafters of

All set and ready to "Rock the Boat". All the guests having a fabulous time!

the two-story height space. At the base of the sails were the boats—silent auction tables created with four eight-foot tables covered in linen. It was a dramatic and inviting space. So many parents said they didn't recognize the place. The intention to do something different was also expressed in the space—from the transformed entrance to the surprising and striking décor that elicited "wows." Plus, we kept the costs low with sails lent by parents, tables in the community center, and just rented the tablecloths and the pipe and drape for the entrance foyer.

To practice **Event Design**, start by noticing—paying attention—to your surroundings. From the moment I begin working with a client, I start to envision what their event will look like and what it will FEEL like. I also keep in mind that the event and the space need to reflect the identity of the client. The more clearly I can envision the space and the event, the better I can manifest the desired result. This happens over time as the foundation is clarified and built.

Before you begin planning, do some informal research on different environments. As my friend, Faye, a wellness coach, says, *"Our body is an antenna, constantly giving and receiving guiding signals."* Notice how it feels when you walk into different spaces. How are they arranged? What colors are used? My intention when designing spaces for events is to have them be welcoming, inviting, and soothing to the body. What does that mean? Here are questions to consider:

- How does it feel when you walk into a space that is all neutral colors?
- How does it feel when there are lots of bright colors?

Everything is an Event 13

- How does it feel when you walk into a space that is a big jumble of furniture and other things?
- How does it feel in an orderly, clean, and simple space?

If you have ever been to a spa, you would probably say that the space feels relaxing and calming, right? I bet there are neutral colors, soft lighting, and comfortable furniture that set a soothing mood.

I'm sure you are aware of having a gut reaction, right? That could be about someone you meet, or it could be about a space you walked into. Notice your gut reaction. Notice what spaces feel like when you walk into them. This will help you with designing your event.

I invite you to try this **exercise** I call **Looking Through the Eyes of the Guest.** This may help you to change how you think about entertaining and planning any kind of gathering or event.

> For the sake of this exercise, let's say you are hosting a summer dinner party, a BBQ, in your home for twelve people. You have planned a menu and prepped all the food. Beverages and glasses are arranged on a table for the bar, allowing easy access for your guests. Some hors d'oeuvres are set out on the coffee table or on a table outside, the buffet is set with all the plates, flatware is wrapped in napkins in a basket, and all is ready for when it's time to bring out the food for dinner. The house is sparkling with fresh flowers arranged. You are ready to welcome your guests
>
> Now, I want you to step into your guests' shoes. In your mind's eye—to go outside and walk up to your front door. You are now a guest arriving at your party. You arrive at the front door and see a beautiful pot of flowers by the door welcoming you. You ring the bell and are welcomed warmly by the host. Already, you feel happy to be there. You put your coat in the bedroom down the hall as your host suggests, and they invite you to choose a beverage at the bar. Your host introduces you to other guests, and you see someone you know. You feel relaxed joining the other guests. You help yourself to some delicious hors d'oeuvres your host has set out. You notice how easy it is to find your way—to the beverages, to chat with others. Or you notice that there is a chair in the way of getting out to the deck. The point here is to notice the flow—is

it easy to move around and through the space? Is it clear where to go? As the evening progresses, you enjoy a wonderful meal, great conversation, and a fabulous dessert. There's lots of laughter and you have enjoyed yourself and made some new friends. You thank your host for a fun evening and depart—so glad you came!

Anything you saw—or experienced—with new eyes? As the host, you are holding the intention that your guests feel welcomed and at ease.

I do this exercise with every event to experience what the event space will feel like before the event. What does my antenna pick up? Is there ease and flow through the space? Is there a place where I stop and wonder which way to go? Is there flow for the timing of each aspect of the event—from cocktails and hors d'oeuvres to dinner, dessert, and more? Are there directional signs needed at certain places? **It's keeping the questions in mind that is most important**.

PRINCIPLE #4:
BE AWARE OF THE FLOW

There are three kinds of flow for an event:

1) Flow and ease of movement through the physical space—allowing guests to move easily and effortlessly through and around the event space.

2) The flow of the timing of the event—one activity or action moves smoothly to the next—as it moves from the guests arriving, through every aspect and action during the event and as guests depart.

3) The flow of the planning process—the qualities of ease, fun, order, etc. must be part of the planning process, not just the end result. Walking the talk throughout all aspects of the event. Outlining the timing of what needs to be accomplished when provides order and ease in accomplishing all the aspects of the event.

In designing your event, be aware of these aspects of flow.

Everything is an Event

PRINCIPLE #5:
CLARITY OF INTENTION

Being clear about your intention for your event is essential to manifesting the event you envision and desire. Intention is a fundamental factor in creating success—in any domain of our life and especially for events. **How you THINK about your event is the real key to event planning.** *When you have passion for what you are planning, your passion fuels your intention.*

An event planner's job is to hold the intention and purpose foremost in mind during all planning and coordinating.

There are two principles that support this:

PRINCIPLE #6:
WHAT YOU FOCUS ON INCREASES

PRINCIPLE #7:
WHEN YOU PLACE YOUR *ATTENTION* ON YOUR *INTENTION*—WITH CLARITY OF PURPOSE—YOU CAN MANIFEST THE DESIRED RESULT

Working with clients, the first thing I do is clarify the intention and purpose of their event. They may be different than what they think. And throughout the planning process, I continue to remind them of their intention and hold that intention for them. Every detail must be looked at to make sure it is coherent with the event's purpose.

When I was invited to help plan the school auction, I began to hear stories about the previous years' auctions. What I heard from parents was that in previous years, they had been told that they HAD to attend the school auction, and they HAD to spend money. That didn't sound inviting to me. I certainly wouldn't have wanted to attend. So, I first began to clarify with the committee why we put on this auction event every year. I declared that our purpose and intention was "to have fun and create community"—to create connection with all the parents. When someone would bring up that we needed to raise money, I would repeat, "Our goal, our intention, is *to have fun and create community*." I was a broken record, repeating this over and over. You know what happened? The event was SO much fun—everyone was buzzing about it for weeks and weeks afterward, and thus the event grew each year. As this was a volunteer committee, there was a very modest budget. Parents were willing to pitch in and donate their time and materials wherever possible. The more volunteers who participated, the more people were focused on the same goal and going in the same direction, thus increasing the potential for success. **What you focus on increases.**

As the host, you are holding the intention that your guests feel welcomed and at ease.

PRINCIPLE #8:
WHEN YOU HAVE FUN AND CREATE COMMUNITY, THE MEMORIES WILL FOLLOW
THE MONEY WILL FOLLOW
THE BUZZ WILL FOLLOW

Fun is the energy of attraction. **Community** is coming together in unity—unity of purpose. All guests are there for the same purpose. By building relationships, there is the possibility of help in many forms, not just money, and you open up to receiving more.

Maybe you volunteer at a nonprofit and help with their annual event, or you are on the board of a nonprofit, or you volunteer for your school fundraiser. I know "fund" is in that word, but it is misleading. When my nonprofit clients or large organizations say they want to plan a fundraising event to raise money for their organization, I explain that that is not the purpose of their event and will not provide the desired result. Why?

You Can't Invite Money to a Party

You invite people. It is about building relationships. With the intention of building relationships, you open up a wider net to receive more. Money is a by-product of the event, not the purpose.

The event really is a **FUNraiser and a FRIENDraiser**.

Everything is an Event

For each event, there is a purpose and reason to host the event. If the event is a wedding, the purpose is to bring together family and friends to celebrate the couple and their marriage. A milestone birthday, such as a fiftieth or sixtieth birthday, is reason to gather and celebrate that milestone. If it's a backyard barbeque, all are there to socialize with friends, old and new, enjoy good food . . . and have fun doing so. If it's a school auction, everyone there wants to support their children and their school, and . . . when you are having fun, you can't help but spend money on the auction. A corporate event to entertain clients is intended to appreciate the clients and build relationships. If it is a product launch, the company is inviting their most important clients and press to learn about their new product and build relationships.

In defining the intention for an event, it is important to clarify what you want the **atmosphere** to be and what you want your guests to **experience**.

What every guest will talk about is their experience of the party—not how the tables were arranged or what the lighting looked like. They will talk about how the event made them feel. Isn't that what you talk about after leaving an event? How much fun you had? Or how impressed you were with the organization? Or that event was a WOW—and you don't want to miss it next year, plus you want to make sure your friends come, too?

I helped a client host a party for about 100 neighbors and friends in their home to celebrate their recent marriage. The guests were well taken care of—they were greeted at the door, invited to have a beverage, and fed well on delicious hors d'oeuvres, a buffet supper, and a special cake as well as entertained with a wonderful band playing lively music. It wasn't the parts that made this a success. It was the intention at the start of the planning to design the event according to the experience my clients wanted their guests to have: a feeling of connection, community, celebration, fun, and for it to be beautiful, relaxed, and elegant. What did the guests say about the evening? It was the best party they had ever attended!

. . . .

A client wanted to host a special sixtieth birthday party. The '60s was the theme, and a fun celebration was the purpose. The space was decorated with '60s flower power décor, tables filled with round sunglasses and love beads. I had tie-dye T-shirts and headbands created for every guest. T-shirts were draped over the chairs at the dinner tables, and the headbands with ribbon ties were wrapped around the napkins. There was a wig "bar" where anyone could add a long wig or

The colorful setting ready for the guests to celebrate the host's 60th Birthday. Tie-dyed T-shirts for each guest placed over the backs of the chairs and headbands with ribbons wrapped around the napkins. A delicious flower-power cake displayed, the wig and mustache bar, and Marinda dressed for the occasion

add a mustache. When you commit to a theme, go for it! Your guests will embrace the fun! Needless to say, guests put on the wigs and the T-shirts. Dinner was served at the tables, and the flower power birthday cake was delicious. I had to add a headband and glasses to my look to keep with the theme. The band was great and got everyone up dancing. A super fun time was had by all!

When I help plan any event, I am clear that my job is to **create the container** within which the event will occur. That's your job, too! With the information in this book, you will be the event planner for your events. First, hold your vision of your purpose and goals—or the vision of your client's purpose and goals, and second, create the atmosphere and the experience the guests walk into. For every event, I know I want to make sure the guests feel appreciated and taken care of. Don't you want that, too?

Have you ever walked into a party . . . and said to yourself,
Oh, wow, this is fun!?
Was there a sign at the door that said this?
No?

Everything is an Event 19

You were reading the energy of the space, the atmosphere.

I call this the **Energy Bubble** you walked into.

What kind of experience do you want your guests to have? What qualities do you want expressed? This is where I begin to "build" the atmosphere—**the Energy Bubble**. Every thought, every action you take, is building the atmosphere that guests walk into. Being mindful of this will keep you on track.

PRINCIPLE #9:
BUILD THE ATMOSPHERE

Here's an exercise to help you start visualizing what you want your guests to experience at your event. The first Energy Bubble illustration shows an example of what qualities you might want your guests to experience. The second illustration is blank so you can fill it in for your specific event. Remember, you want to clarify what qualities you want your guests to experience. These are NOT things you arrange the space with.

When I work with wedding clients especially, I start by asking them what qualities they want to experience on their wedding day and what qualities they want their guests to experience. Why do I ask wedding clients this question? I find that many start picturing the day, the space, the decorations, the details. It is important to first clarify these qualities to build a foundation upon; every other thought, action, and detail supports the initial intention.

As Maya Angelou said,

"I've learned that people will forget what you said, people will forget what you did, but people will never forget how you made them feel."

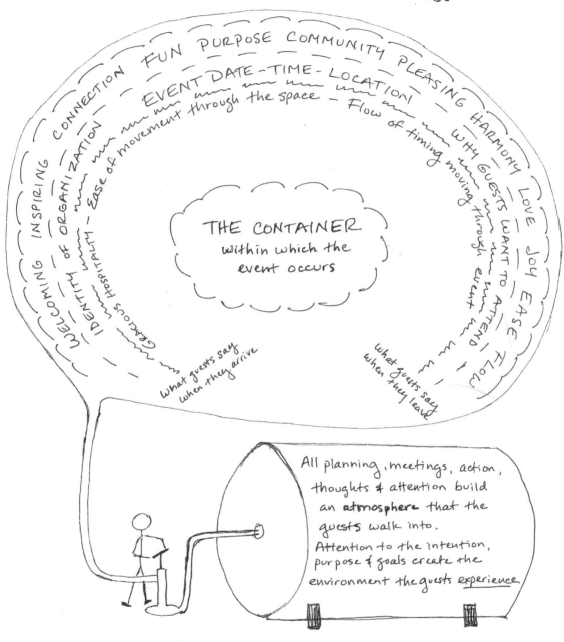

Everything is an Event 21

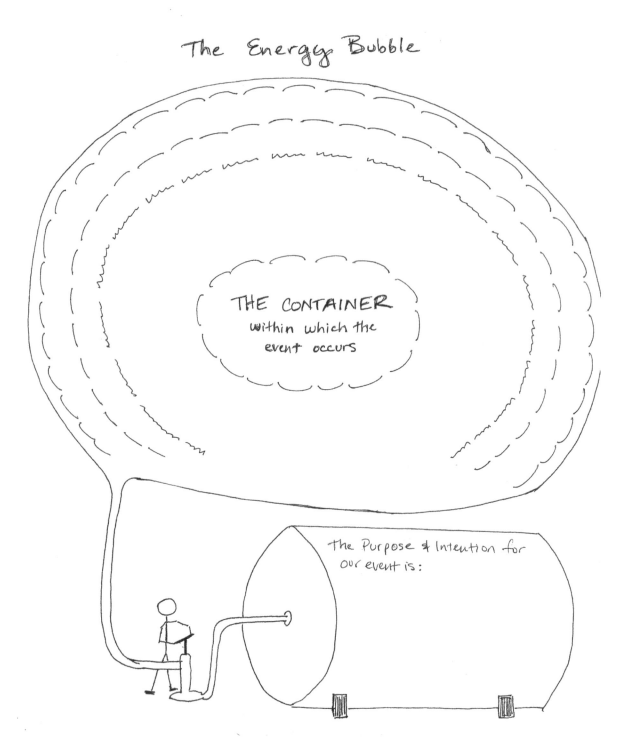

Here's the Energy Bubble for you to fill out. Make copies and write your clear purpose and intention for your event in the tank. Fill in the Bubble with the qualities you want your guests to experience.

Everything is an Event

I coordinated a small wedding for about forty friends held in a redwood grove picnic area. The qualities the bride and groom desired to experience for their day were fun, happiness, joy, love, authenticity, celebration, family, friendship, and connection in a relaxed, comfortable, casual atmosphere. They created and sent out a lovely flyer for their wedding invitation—certainly emphasizing a casual yet still special celebration.

The redwood grove had three long rows of rough wooden picnic tables. The area was in the shade of tall redwood trees, and the space felt very dark. On the day of the wedding, the space was transformed, and it was done very simply. The cream linen tablecloths on the long tables with potted ivy and white flowering plants down the center lightened the space. The change created a feeling in the guests that said special wedding. The ceremony and the connections of the guests with the bride and groom had a feeling of intimacy. The guests could not stop exclaiming over the beautiful space. One table was set up with guest book pages and Sharpies for each guest to write a message for the bride and groom. The pages were later put together in a special book for a lovely remembrance of the day. The buffet was prepped and ready for the guests to bring their potluck dishes. A delicious meal was enjoyed by all—especially the beautiful cake made by a friend of the bride and groom with white icing and decorated with fresh strawberries.

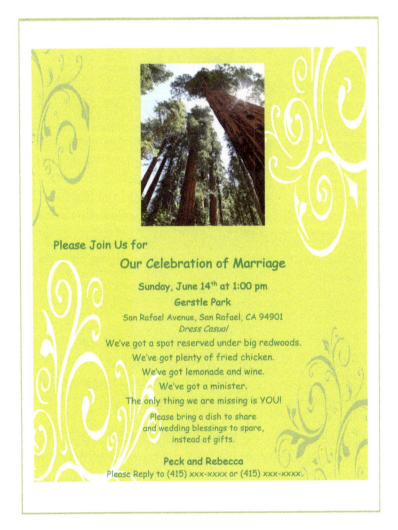

Everything is an Event 23

Before in the redwood grove, after with tables dressed with linen, potted ivy and flowering plants. First slice of cake for Peck & Rebecca, all the plants placed in matching pots and saucers, Marinda managing the event!

The experience the guests had mirrored the qualities the bride and groom had wanted for the day. In fact, many guests said it was one of the best weddings they had ever attended. Years later, one guest reminded me about the amazing wedding experience she had that day. The intangible experience is what guests took away with them and continued to remember.

. . . .

The good news is you can design your event to have the atmosphere, the experience, you intend no matter what kind of event it is. For me, it is important that my clients and I have fun as we plan the event and that the guests have fun at the event. **Fun is the energy of attraction.** Don't we all want to be where the fun is?

Of course, not all events are meant to be fun. Memorials or celebrations of life don't have that intention; however, they do have the intention of bringing people together to share their love for the deceased and remember them. The intimacy of a memorial with hearts open in shared grief brings everyone together in an atmosphere of love and celebration of that special person who had been in their lives.

Baby blessings and baby naming ceremonies are joyful celebrations. All are coming together in unity—community—with the purpose to rejoice in the arrival of a new being.

PRINCIPLE #10:
ORDER CREATES GREATER CALM AND PEACE OF MIND

Order is required for planning and producing any event. The next chapters outline the tools to use and the path to take to create order so you can think clearly about your event and ensure that every detail is taken care of way before your event takes place. There is a process to stay organized during all your planning and at your event. If you do your homework, as defined in this book, it will allow you to breathe, release worry, and relax. Sound impossible? It's really not.

Plus, I always claim ease—ease in planning and ease during the event. I invite you to do the same. Why not?

Here's a way to visualize the order you create to produce your event. All these aspects surrounding the event are important to your success. The Mantras are your thoughts and how you think about what you envision. The Flow is explained on page 15. Chapter Two and Four will explain the tools required for order and ease of planning and production. Review Chapter One again for the Purpose for your event and Atmosphere you design - both important!

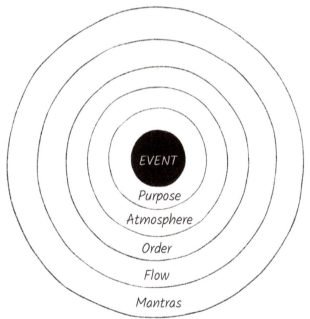

My hope is that this book provides the tools you need to plan your events with ease and peace of mind ...

Everything is an Event 25

"To be a designer is to be an agent of change."

–Daniel Pink, *A Whole New Mind*

Chapter Two

The Essential Elements–
Tools to Build Your Event

There are tools that are essential for any event you want to plan. By using these tools, you will create order, and **order creates greater calm and peace of mind—PRINCIPLE #10.**

Did I mention that planning an event means planning ahead? If you are helping with an annual event, start nine to ten months in advance. As I tell my clients, there's a reason gestation is nine months. This allows you to think clearly about all the actions required and all the people you need to contact and confirm, plus you aren't pressed to do everything at the last minute—which is a recipe for disaster and so not necessary. If the event is much smaller, still give yourself a few months, not weeks! People are busy. If it's a dinner party in your home, a month or two is probably fine. I host an Academy Awards party every year, and I send out my invitation in early January for the usual end-of-February date. I wait till after the holidays to send it. Be kind and give your guests advance notice to get the date on their calendar.

Some basic tools for planning your event are:

- Event checklist
- Event binder
- Event Timeline
- Budget
- Folders in your computer—mirroring the tabs in your binder
- Program schedule
- Floor plan or map
- Staffing schedule
- Vendor List

The first thing I do is create a binder. Yes, a physical binder with tabs. You are creating a physical event, and you need all the information at your fingertips. Yes, I also create folders on my computer that mirror those in the binder. You need both! You cannot rely on the internet to work to look up anything when you are on-site, so plan ahead and have all important information printed, in your binder, and on your event clipboard. I also find that reviewing the different tabs in my binder helps me to look at all the pieces being put together and ensures I am not forgetting something.

Remember, there is research required . . . .

The tabs I always put in my binder are in this order:

CONTACTS: This could be a committee's names, phones and emails, or other contacts you need—location, caterer, other vendors, etc. All in one place.

NOTES: With every call and meeting, there are notes to take about event specifics. Write it all down. Who can keep it all in your head? I can't! When I manage a meeting with a volunteer committee, I provide a meeting agenda and then write up the notes so there is a record of what occurred. Then I email the notes to the committee.

BUDGET: Start building a budget. Contact the vendors, get estimates, and plug these into your budget document. This can be a simple Excel document. I list all the expense items and then have two columns—one for estimate and a second for actual, to be filled in as the event is finalized. As your planning moves forward, keep updating the budget. Only when you have researched costs, can you get a clear idea of what the total cost of your event is and therefore, determine what you absolutely must have for your event. Sharpen your pencil and think about what is most cost-effective for your envisioned effect.

LOCATION: You need a place to hold your event, right? Whether it's an event rental location, a private home, a hotel, or some other place, you need to secure the space. It could even be a picnic area that you need to reserve in advance. The location is one of the first things you need to confirm when beginning to plan the specifics. The date also needs to be established. The date may be determined by the availability of the space.

TIMELINES: There are two different timelines that help create order in planning and producing your event.

> **1) Project Timeline**: For most large events that have many months of planning, I create a project timeline. This is a schedule estimating when each item needs to get done. To get this started, begin at the end and work backward. Put in all your meeting dates, including the review meeting after your event. I do this in

an Excel spreadsheet with a column on the left for the date due and a column next where I put in the actual date so I can track what really happens. The next column is the action description and the final column lists who is doing this action. If you plan an annual event, you can keep updating this each year. This helps you have the big picture in mind.

2) Event Timeline: As you get closer to the event—a couple of months out or so—start your event timeline. This includes prep a day or two or three before the event as you collect items, then there's load-in, setup, the event, and breakdown. **This is one of the most important documents you create. It's a road map for your event.** Do this for every event, really. If you are planning a dinner party or your Thanksgiving dinner, write out all actions and timing leading up to the dinner. This includes when you do shopping, ordering rental dishes if need be, prepping food, baking pies, setting the table the day before, and then day-of prep and cooking. Put it all down so you can see when you need to do what. No need to try and keep all these details in your head. I can't! This is the key document that provides order, which equals greater calm and peace of mind for you!

There are more specifics for this important tool later on in this book.

MAP: Also known as a floor plan. In a room or space in a building, you need a floor plan. When I plan a large outdoor event such as a 5K walk/run or festival, it's a map. This is an important element for planning and visualizing your event in the space.

FOOD AND BEVERAGES: This can be the food and beverages you provide when you entertain at home, or it can be a caterer you hire for a larger event. Let's address home entertaining first.

HOME ENTERTAINING: I always write down my menu when entertaining guests in my home. It is important to design a menu that gets you out of the kitchen when your guests are present. There are so many things you can serve that you can prepare in advance. If I have a summer party, I love to serve grilled food. However, I start grilling four to five hours in advance so that all the food is grilled and arranged on platters way before the guests arrive. I'll grill marinated chicken, thick slices of onion, eggplant, yellow squash, and carrots. I love grilled carrots and so do my guests. The trick to grilling carrots is to start them over the heat and then move them to the other side of the grill away from the direct heat to continue cooking (with the lid down) until they are done. The fresh mixed green salad is prepped and ready in the fridge, just waiting till it's time to be tossed with the vinaigrette at the last minute.

Everything is an Event

With a grilling menu, grilled peaches and coconut sorbet are an easy dessert.

I'll provide some other menu suggestions later in the Appendix. This is just to get you thinking with this example.

CATERER: A caterer is invaluable for larger events. My rule of thumb with catering is to consider that food is fifty percent of the cost and staff is the other fifty percent. Staff can provide food service and bartending. If you don't have enough staff, it doesn't matter how good the food is. You need guests taken care of, dishes and glasses picked up so that guests don't notice there's a mess anywhere. They will only notice this when you don't have enough staff. Trust me on this one.

RENTALS: Unless it's a small party in your home and you have all the dishes, you will need to rent dishes, linen, tables, etc. The space will dictate what is required. Many locations provide tables and chairs, which can be a cost savings.

VENDORS: AV, lighting, décor—what vendors you need depends on the event you are planning. AV (audiovisual) rentals usually include a sound system. You may need a projector and screen. Lighting is a very cost-effective way to decorate a space. Companies that specialize in lighting know how to do this. Decorations can be simple or more elaborate, again determined by your event. A tip about linen color to keep in mind—choose ONE color of linen. It is easier on the eye to have one color rather than a mix and, having one color ties the space together visually.

I did a wedding on top of a mountain in Sonoma County—a picturesque space for an afternoon/evening wedding—except there was no lighting. I hired a lighting company to provide lights so that all could see—most importantly, safety first. All the large white paper globes strung across the wedding space were also a beautiful

The outdoor setting ready for the Wedding Reception with globe lighting set up around the property for décor and safety when it gets dark. The Bride and Groom, Carmen and Elmo.

A beautiful, colorful bridal bouquet. After the ceremony, the Bride and Groom celebrate in the California country setting with summer golden hills and an antique tractor.

décor element. With the burgundy linen on all the tables and local dahlias for centerpieces, it created a striking setting for the reception.

BAND/MUSIC: Music sets a mood. When a guest walks into the space, music fills the space with welcoming energy much more than a quiet room does. It's definitely more inviting. Live music has more energy than recorded music, but it depends on what is needed for the event. You don't just arrange a beautiful space with ease and flow, the sound of music dresses up the space in an intangible way. In my home, I have speakers in the living room, kitchen, and dining room so I can have beautiful music playing when I entertain or just for me to enjoy.

STAFF: Whether you hire staff or have a volunteer staff, you will need to have a plan for what staff you need and what their roles are. Clarity again! If you hire a caterer, they will provide the staff. My personal rule for home entertaining is if the guest count is over twenty, I hire staff. Otherwise, I will be constantly working—setting out food, serving, and cleaning up—and then I won't have the time to spend with my guests.

ANOTHER NOTE ABOUT STAFF: With large events where more staff is needed, it is important to know who to call to get staff. **As an event professional, my job is not to know everything, just who to call to get what I need**.

PRINTED MATERIALS: This may include flyers, website design and updates, invitations, programs, signs, and more. **Consistency of branding**, whether it is a wedding, a gala fundraiser, or a special party, helps identify the event for those

Everything is an Event 33

invited. It's best for all the components—the flyer, invitation, program, escort cards, place cards, name tags, etc.—to all have the same look. A good graphic designer can be a huge help with this. Of course, there are lots of sources for graphics on the Internet, too. Keep it simple and consistent!

INSURANCE: Most rental spaces require event insurance. This does not have to be a big expense. If you are planning a big event, you will probably need an ABC license for serving liquor. Again, it depends. You can usually get an event rider from your insurance agent.

MARKETING: It is important to keep in mind that consistency of visuals is always a good idea whether it is a wedding, a special celebration, or even a memorial. It's a way of tying the elements together visually. If the event needs to be promoted, marketing could include flyers, advertising, website promotion, social media, and mailings.

For larger events or different kinds of events, I have other tabs in my binders. These events have included weddings, major birthday celebrations, nonprofit events, gala fundraisers, conferences, walks, and more. Other tabs I have added to many of my binders include **speakers, sponsors, program, invitation list, attendee list, press and more.**

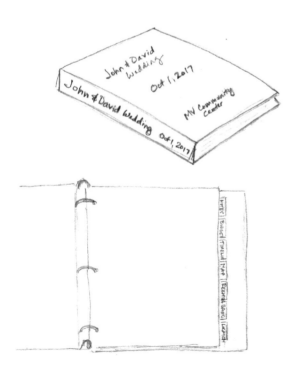

The tabs needed in your binder will be determined by what is required for your event. Each little detail can have many parts to it. For example, I plan and coordinate an annual conference where one element is speaker gifts, which are chosen by the committee, and I place the order. Then the gifts are wrapped, put in gift bags, and personalized gift cards are tied on each bag. So, ribbon, wrapping paper and gift bags need to be purchased and gift cards printed. Fifty to seventy-five gifts take some time to assemble and wrap. If you've ever helped with a large gala event where the guests are given a gift bag as they depart, you know that filling 400 or so bags requires an orderly assembly line.

PRINCIPLE #11:
SMALL DETAILS CAN EQUAL BIG CONSEQUENCES

Have you ever received a gift bag as you departed an event? Didn't it make you feel great to know that they thought about you and wanted to thank you for coming?

Another example of a small detail for an annual conference is that we need the speaker information, their photo, bio, presentation title, and description in November, before we open registration in December, so we can ask registrants which sessions they are most interested in. This information will be used months later when we determine which meeting rooms to place the speakers in for the conference. Some rooms are very large, and others are smaller. Best not to have a room for 160 with just a few attendees listening to the speaker.

There are many other instances where a little detail is more than it seems. See what you notice with small details and how they make a big difference!

· ·

A MEMORIAL, A CELEBRATION OF LIFE
AN EXAMPLE OF PLANNING AND ADJUSTING

I helped my friend, Hilda, plan a memorial for her long-time partner, Tim. While l like to plan ahead, it's not always possible for every event. Hilda found a place for the memorial—a small local community center on the mountain near her home. Two weeks before the memorial, we were able to go look at the space she had reserved. I recommended how to set up the space for the ceremony and suggested that the reception that followed be set up on the patio with a beautiful view of the mountain. I noted that they had plenty of tables and seventy-nine folding chairs plus some outdoor furniture. Many friends and family offered to help and bring food.

I suggested that having live music would be nice and more enlivening. She immediately said yes. I called a guitarist friend to see if he was available. He wasn't but I found another guitarist who was available, willing to come, and his partner was happy to come along and play violin. I reviewed some next steps for Hilda to take—order a few rental items, such as pitchers for water and iced tea, clarify who's speaking during the ceremony, order wine and beverages, and other details. We set up a date to meet in a week in my office to review everything.

Everything is an Event

When we met, Hilda had done her homework. She brought an outline of the ceremony program; a list of food being provided and a list of those that could come early to help. Together, we reviewed the order and crafted a flow for the ceremony—who would be speaking when, with a musical interlude in the middle with music by Tim's friends playing songs on guitar and saxophone, and another friend to play a song on the piano to close the ceremony. Then I created the event timeline, listing everything in the ceremony, and added who would be arriving at what time and what help they were providing—directing parking, setting up chairs, tables, and outdoor umbrellas, coordinating the food being brought, who would help clean up, etc., plus first arrivals to help put out the signs and balloons along the road to direct people to the community center.

I printed out a floor plan of the community center from their website and we re-evaluated the best way to set up the space. The plan was for the folding chairs to be arranged in a semi-circle radiating out from the fireplace where people would speak. (Note that setting chairs in a semi-circle instead of straight rows allows guests to see each other and feel more connected.) A table by the door for name tags. A large photo of Tim and flowers would be on the mantel, and there would be two tables with photographs—one inside and one on the patio. Also on the patio would be the buffet of finger foods and a bar with wine, sparkling mineral water, and lemon verbena iced tea. I offered to bring cream-colored tablecloths for all the tables. After the ceremony inside, everyone would be invited outside to the reception. The plan for the guitarist and violinist was to play for an hour while people arrived and then for two hours after the ceremony during the reception.

Hilda and I reviewed the menu—what people had committed to bring and what was needed to fill in for hors d'oeuvres and finger foods. Hilda was then ready to make calls to others and let them know what they could bring. I call this an orchestrated potluck. It's designed to have a balance of foods and make sure there's something for everyone from vegetarians to meat eaters. Our meeting ended with a finalized event timeline, a menu, and a list of who was bringing what—from food to rentals to ice. Hilda said she had been in overwhelm trying to plan the memorial until I stepped in to help. She felt so much more relaxed and at ease. I know it's because order creates greater calm and peace of mind. And yes, I've been planning events for a long time, so I can put it together quickly if needed. (I organized my second wedding for twenty-five guests in one week—but that's another story.) My hope is that this book provides the tools you need to plan your events with ease and peace of mind, just like I helped Hilda.

On Wednesday, before the memorial on Sunday, Hilda and I arranged a phone meeting for an update. Hilda had texted me the day before: "I emailed a second e-vite with directions to the location and a brief schedule of the afternoon. Yikes! Ninety-five people said yes!" I texted back, "Standing room only. It will be wonderful." On the phone, she told me that getting my text made her feel it was all fine that so many were coming, and that she didn't have to worry about it. I said that it is even better that so many are coming—what a gift that so many want to gather to celebrate Tim.

I texted Hilda the morning of the memorial, "No need to put up the three umbrellas as it's cold and windy—twenty degrees cooler than yesterday, and the fog is pouring in over the mountain." "Don't worry," I texted. "I've got a plan." "Okay, I won't worry," she texted back. Before I even got to the community center, I had figured out a new plan to arrange the tables for food and the bar inside. There was a table for photos and mementos and another table for the guest book. A large photo of Tim was on the mantel flanked by beautiful flowers. Yes, there was standing room only. It was a wonderful heartfelt celebration with family and friends sharing their stories about Tim.

Once the ceremony was over, most of the chairs were removed so guests could gather and visit in the same room. It's called "turning the room"—from one setting to another. It just takes a few minutes, especially with many hands to help remove the chairs. The reception allowed family and friends to reconnect. The guitar and violin provided a wonderful background of elegant sound during the two-hour reception. All the food provided was perfect and enjoyed by all. The biggest hit was the pulled pork sandwiches on Hawaiian rolls with aioli made by Tim's son. He made it because it was his dad's favorite. It was a true labor of love as he smoked the meat for twenty hours. Everyone so appreciated the opportunity to gather together to remember Tim, and many people contacted Hilda for days afterward with appreciative remarks such as:

> "It was beautiful and fun to see so many family members and friends, probably the best celebration of life I have been to."

> "Beautiful and inspiring."

"Tim couldn't have asked for a better celebration of life than what you organized for him."

"A most beautiful celebration of life for a most beautiful soul. Well done, well done!"

"Lovely celebration and wonderful opportunity to reconnect."

The intention to bring people together to remember Tim created an atmosphere of love and remembrance that was palpable. Several guests came over to me to thank me for helping to give the gift of the day to all who attended, especially for Hilda.

1) Setting up the altar, 2) Prepping the bar, 3) The table with photos and mementos, 4) Musicians playing during the reception after the memorial.

38 *Everything is an Event*

Tim's Event Timeline

HERE IS AN EXAMPLE OF THE EVENT TIMELINE FOR TIM'S CELEBRATION OF LIFE.

10:30 a.m.	Marinda arrives—brings ice buckets with scoops, verbena iced tea, bar towels, linen tablecloths, pedestals/risers (for buffet), trays, baskets—reserved signs for front row of chairs, Tim's fave signs—for Ruffles potato chips and grapes
	Hilda arrives with wine, mineral water, food, umbrellas/stands, sandbags, pitchers & sister, Patrice
	Patrick arrives with Franco, Terese, & Cousin (brings meats, bread, spread, & spreaders) (Patrick Cell: xxx-xxx-xxxx)
	Patrick & Franco put out directional signs and balloons on road, then help with setup of chairs and tables
11:00 a.m.	Betsy brings flowers & ice, Brooke brings food (Brooke & Betsy receive food brought)
12:00 p.m.	Robert & Susan arrive—set up to play guitar & violin (Susan Cell: xxx-xxx-xxxx)
	Erica, Adam, & kids arrive. Allen, Jim, & Rama arrive
12:15 p.m.	<u>Car parking volunteers ready</u>—Patrick, Franco, & Cousin
12:30 p.m.	Guests begin to arrive, music begins to play—Geri to staff name tag table
	Beverages: lemon verbena iced tea, sparkling & still water w/ lemons at kitchen bar/counter
1:20 p.m.	MC asks guests to be seated for ceremony
1:30 p.m.	**Ceremony begins**
	MC opens ceremony with two readings and centering prayer
1:32 p.m.	Family speakers—Hilda, Rama, Terese, Patrick, Erica (four min. each). Each to introduce the next speaker
2:10 p.m.	MC introduces Musical Interlude—Allen/guitar, Jim/Sax—three songs
2:25 p.m.	MC invites friends to come forward to speak—Mike from Toastmasters first, then invites other guests up to front
	Food put on buffet tables, bar beverages ready (Betsy, Brooke, Cousin, Patty)

Everything is an Event

3:00 p.m.	**Ceremony concludes**—MC to close with reading and prayer. Invite guests to stay for reception
	Robert & Susan to begin playing again
	Guests to help themselves to food and beverages
	A few helpers, Franco, Marty, & Jim, remove most of ceremony folding chairs—leave some in groupings around the room (Marinda to direct)—opening up the room for the reception
5:00 p.m.	**Reception concludes**
	Robert & Susan pack up and depart
	Breakdown—Franco, Patrick, & Cousin put all chairs & tables back in storage area, umbrellas broken down & in Hilda's car plus rentals/food; Veronica, Betsy, & Brooke—food wrapped up and removed, beverages, etc. removed, fold up tablecloths. Load out, take trash
6:00 p.m.	Hilda & Marinda lock up

Celebration of Life to Honor Tim Driscoll

June 24, 2018

Muir Woods Park Community Center
Mill Valley, California

October 29, 1944 – February 22, 2018

1:30 – 2:30 pm – Ceremony
2:30 – 4:30 pm – Celebration

On behalf of the Driscoll Family and Hilda Leefeldt, we wish to thank you for your kind thoughts and support - and for joining us today in celebration of Tim's wonderful life.

"Climb the mountains and get their good tidings. Nature's peace will flow into you as sunshine flows into trees. The winds will blow their own freshness into you, and the storms their energy, while cares will drop away like autumn leaves."   ~ John Muir

"I only went out for a walk and finally concluded to stay out till sundown, for going out, I found, was really going in."
~ John Muir

There are those who possess a light so bright it not only lights their way, but guides others as well. Even in darkness, Tim's light will continue to shine through every heart he touched.

An Irish Blessing
"May the road rise up to meet you. May the wind be always at your back. May the sun shine warm upon your face, the rains fall soft upon your fields, and until we meet again, may God hold you in the palm of his hand."

Special thanks to Marinda Freeman of MF Productions for her generous help in planning this celebration, and to the musicians who played for us: Allen Klein, Jim Argo, Vince Darling, and Robert Adamich and Susan Schloss.

40 *Everything is an Event*

"If you change the way you look at things, the things you look at change."

–Wayne Dyer

Chapter Three

Mantras and Words to Live By

What I believe no one tells you is that planning an event is really about noticing and managing the conversations in your head. Panic and stress are about the stories you have stirred up in your thoughts that are now racing and running you. This is not necessary. Truly. You could call this mindfulness, which is really just paying attention to your mind and your thoughts.

PRINCIPLE #12:
HOW YOU THINK COMES BEFORE HOW YOU TAKE ACTION

I have found that it is essential to be aware of my inner conversations when planning events. Are you aware of your inner conversation? If your thoughts are going south, do you have a way to replace them with something better? Listed below are ways to look at and think about your event, as well as to hold the vision and stay focused on the intentions for your event.

And remember . . .

> *your intention is what fuels your interest and desire to produce the perfect event you envision.*

Do these thoughts sound familiar?

I am so overwhelmed. I'm never going to get this done. I don't know how to do this. I should never have started this. How did I get talked into doing this?! This is just too stressful for me. What if nobody comes? What am I going to make for the food? Will it taste good? Will people have a good time? Will everyone get along?

What I call mantras could also be called words to live by. For me, a mantra is a statement that I focus my attention on and repeat over and over. The *Merriam-Webster Dictionary* defines mantra as "a word or phrase that is repeated often or that expresses someone's basic beliefs."

My list of mantras grew over time as I learned more about the event principles that are always operating. I have repeated these over and over—to remind myself of these truths and thus how to think about the planning and actions required. I found that these mantras help me stay focused on the big picture—the macro—while also addressing the details—the micro—that support the big picture. Perhaps these will ring true for you.

CONNECTING THE DOTS

Connecting the dots is making sure that each step is thought through from beginning to end. Start at the beginning of your event and walk through to the end. For example, you ordered flowers and arranged for delivery at a certain time. What happens after the event is over? Can your guests take the centerpiece? Or can they take the flowers but leave the container? Do you need to return the containers to the florist? Pick any aspect of your event and follow it through. Having an event timeline helps to put it all down on paper so you don't have to remember all the details in your head.

A client of mine described this thought process as connecting a string from the beginning actions running through to the very end after the event. Connecting the dots. Connecting the string. You choose the phrase but think it through!

> **The Case of the Missing Napkins.**
>
> After a gala nonprofit event, there were 2,500 napkins that did not arrive back at the rental company. At $1.40 each, that meant they would have to pay $3,500 to the rental company to cover the loss. Not what a nonprofit wants to spend money on. However, they were finally discovered at another rental company and were returned. Whew! This was a clear lesson in connecting the dots. The following year there were lists for the event managers of what rentals went where at the end of the event so that this wouldn't happen again.

WEAVE THE TAPESTRY . . . HOLD THE THREADS

Creating your event means you take all the pieces you are working on and weave them together to create the whole picture of your event. They are all connected. Maintain the macro view and then zoom into the little details that make a difference. Back to the macro and zoom into the micro, always holding the vision of the finished event tapestry. And, address all those important little details. Many times, those details are ways to express "we care about you" to your guests.

Did you know that people really love getting a printed name tag with their name spelled correctly? It makes them happy. Really. I watched this for years. They are not happy if their name is misspelled. For meetings or conferences, I will print a new corrected name tag, which makes them smile. I bring my laptop and printer with blank name tags so I'm ready for any corrections or new name tags needed. Yes, sometimes people don't want to wear their name tag, but I encourage them to put it on. Remember, the purpose of every event is to create connection. Name tags help people meet each other and remember their names. I need the help, don't you? And it's not just for meetings and conferences. Rehearsal dinners, where people are meeting each other for the first time, are another type of event where name tags can be appropriate. Everyone is coming together for a special celebration—creating a new community. If you have pin name tags and you have guests who don't want to put a pin in their clothing, there are solutions. Have blue painter's tape handy to use folded into a loop. There are also magnetic name tags in several sizes that don't affect someone's clothing.

What if there's no name tag for them? Be prepared. Bring your laptop and printer. Or Sharpies and blank name tags.

For more formal entertaining such as weddings, special celebrations, and dinner parties, make sure your guests' names are spelled correctly on the place cards, escort cards, gift bags, etc. Again, it says you care.

Three examples of escort cards laid out for the guests to pick up and find out which table they are assigned.

Everything is an Event 45

IT WILL BE REVEALED

Sometimes in the planning process, there arises a question there isn't an answer to—yet. It will be revealed . . . as we move along in the process. Once we have the question, keep the question in mind until the answer, the solution, is revealed. Don't be a nag about the question. Just hold it lightly in mind.

It will be revealed. I have found this statement to always be true, and I have taught it to my clients. One volunteer committee I worked with really embraced this belief. Members repeated it at committee planning meetings when some questions arose as we got close to their nonprofit gala event for 500 guests. One example was the question, "How do we finish the entrance decor?"

The gala fundraiser theme was "Come Fly with Us." The entrance had a big multilingual Welcome sign, like at an airport. Saturday morning, event day, the royal blue entrance carpet was installed. I had bought four-inch yellow duct tape to possibly use on the carpet and other items as we were not sure what was needed. The décor team decided to put a double row of yellow tape down the center of the carpet and then continued the tape into the reception area—all the way up to the circular bar. When this was completed, one of the committee members reminded me, "See, it *was* revealed!"

At the start of the gala, ramp directors in white jumpsuits with red safety vests used lighted wands to direct guests down the carpeted runway entrance—as they would for airplanes. Volunteer flight attendants in vintage uniforms welcomed guests as they came aboard. Drinks and hors d'oeuvres were passed for the 500 guests during the reception.

Ramp Director ready to direct the guests into the gala evening. Guests follow the yellow lines into the Cocktail Reception where they are greeted with a beverage and guided to the bar.

46 *Everything is an Event*

The Dining area set and ready for the guests and a close up of a dinner table with paper airplane centerpiece above a cloud covered tablecloth.

When it was time for dinner, lights flashed to cue the flight attendants and ramp directors to direct guests after the announcement from the captain: *"This is your captain speaking. It is now time . . . please take your seats for takeoff and for dinner."*

Have an attitude of curiosity. **Focusing on the questions** that arise when planning an event is especially important.

- Is everything in alignment with my purpose and goals?
- Do all the details support the reason for this event?
- Is there coherence?
- Do all the parts fit together to make an integrated whole?
- Am I continually looking at the macro and the micro—all the details?
- By keeping these and other questions in mind, the answers WILL be revealed.

Remember, all the planning and review you have done, over and over, provides certainty you have covered everything that you have wanted for your event and envisioned the event before the event. Having done so, you can be present, calm, and can think in the moment to solve whatever circumstance or situation arises during the event.

IT WILL ALL GET DONE

I said this a lot to myself in the first years I was planning events. Now, it's a given that every detail, every aspect, will be handled in the most appropriate way. There are still occasions that I repeat this mantra. I get calmer just saying it to myself. I have proved it many times. It does all get done—in its right way and right time. This also means I am still working, taking action to move the event along in its planning process to completion—to the date, time, and place of the event. I also am listening for the right time to take each action.

Many years ago, I coordinated a tenth wedding anniversary party for Liza Minnelli and her then-husband, Marc Gero, in a new New York City restaurant. It was Robert De Niro's restaurant in the meat-packing district at the time when the area was just beginning to change. The restaurant was so new that it wasn't finished. In fact, I spent the two months prior to the event working with the contractors to stay on top of the project and to make sure that the spaces we needed would be done enough in time for the event. This was the only time in my event planning career that I worked with contractors in planning an event. There was no kitchen (the caterer created their own on-site), the heating ducts were not in place, and many other areas were not close to being finished. I really did have to practice repeating my mantra, "It will all get done," with this event!

Because the space wasn't finished, the design team could paint the cement floor in one area and turn it into a black-and-white checkered dance floor. Tables and chairs were dressed with linen in the main room as guests entered, which changed the view so it looked good despite the construction zone behind the scenes. It was down to the wire, with the front door being installed about an hour before show time. The guests thought the restaurant was finished when they walked in, and they were thrilled to be the first ones to see it. A couple of people walked in, not on the guest list, thinking the restaurant had opened. Ah, the art of display and décor. It can definitely change what the guests see, and what they don't see—all that construction was behind the scenes! Yes, it DID all get done and the party was a smash success.

In 2014, I was asked by a long-time client to take on the planning of a free outdoor community event with a focus on water conservation and environmental awareness. When I started, the event had been held for a few years, but there were no records from previous years, so I was basically starting from scratch. And, I had to plan and make this event happen in just four months' time! I know, I say you need nine to ten months of planning for an annual event. Well, there wasn't the time to do that this go-round. Needless to say, it was a push to put everything together, and I used this mantra—"It will all get done." I redesigned the event using Google Earth and my CAD program to make a to-scale map of the whole outdoor area and how the event would be set up. Working with the nonprofit organization's committee, I started a sponsor program to help underwrite costs. They solicited sponsors as they were building relationships with them and their organization. The funds raised from this event provided educational programs for children.

A list was created of people and organizations to invite to have a booth. There were many educational and interactive activities for children and adults from archery to seeing squiggly things in water under microscopes. There were steelhead jumping the fish ladder. There were food trucks, a great band, and a bubble show, which was a huge hit with the kids. The first year, 2015, there were 5,000 that attended. Yes, for the second year, we started the planning in June for the February event, giving more time for planning and thought. The fifth year of the event it had grown to 12,000 children and adults attending. What was the purpose? To provide a free, fun, educational, outdoor experience, and activities for families in the community, as well as to provide greater awareness of fish and water conservation. Build it and they will come, right?

IT IS ALL UNFOLDING PERFECTLY

This mantra ties into the mantra above. It will all get done in its right way and right time, and it is all unfolding perfectly.

Let me clarify what I mean by "perfectly." It's not a judgment about the situation or the event, it's affirming that whatever happens is perfect just the way it is. The way it is IS perfect. Sometimes it's hard to see how that could be the case but holding this idea in mind—keeps my awareness open to what needs to be tended to in each moment. No stressing over this or that. Remember, you are holding the big picture and attending to the details that support the big picture.

Everything is an Event 49

I have more peace when I remind myself of this mantra. With more peace, there is more space to think clearly about the event and all the details—and to listen for guidance.

Years ago, I planned and produced an environmental conference for a nonprofit organization at a lovely location in Napa Valley. Working with a committee, the planning for the one-day conference took place over eight months. Two weeks before the conference, a staff member from the location called me to say that they thought it would be better if we held the event in a local hotel. My response was, "No way is that happening!" Two weeks before the conference?! I reminded them of our contract and that the event would be held as planned. All the speakers had been booked and all had been informed of the location. The planning had been organized and coordinated around that location. I could have gotten really upset or freaked out. Who has time for that?! To me, it just showed how disorganized the location staff were. I knew, in spite of this blip, it was all unfolding perfectly. The conference went off without a hitch at the planned site. Everyone attending had a great time and the client was very happy. The location? They closed down about six months later.

WHAT IS "PERFECT" ANYWAY? A WEDDING STORY

Years ago, I helped my good friend, Kay, with her niece, Hallie's, wedding. Kay had secured a beautiful property for the ceremony and reception. She rented twelve-foot wooden church pews for the ceremony, and with the tall trees surrounding the space, it really felt like a cathedral. All four of Hallie's sisters were bridesmaids, and her groom, Adam, included his friends and Hallie's brother as groomsmen. The large property and small house did not lend themselves to renting a tent, so we just kept an eye on the weather. Set up the day before was a family affair with everyone pitching in to string lights, set up furniture, and prepare the front space for the ceremony and the larger back space for the reception with tables and chairs, furniture groupings, and decorations around the pool.

The afternoon of the wedding everything was ready. Guests had arrived and were seated in the pews. Kay suddenly got a weather alert that a storm cloud was coming, "We have to start the wedding now!" I told the groom and groomsmen it was time to line up. I let the bride and bridesmaids know that we would be starting in just a minute and then it began. The ceremony was beautiful and went off without a hitch. As soon as the bride and groom and wedding party had walked back down the aisle after the ceremony, the skies opened up, and it poured. The bridal party was under cover in the garage. The guests scattered—many into the house. Other guests left, especially those with small children. All the good friends and family stayed. Several of us pulled out the big roll of plastic we had procured "just in case" and started covering the wooden benches. Good thing I was wearing washable silk as I was soaked.

We also had to cover the furniture in the reception area with plastic. It was such a downpour that water was pouring through the property, gushing like a stream. Drinks were being served in the house and garage. Someone went and purchased a few 10x10 popup tents. One went over the DJ, another over the bar. When the rain stopped, it was the perfect time for the first dance. And then everyone joined them on the dance floor and boogied. The rain came again, and people huddled under the tent by the bar, in the house, and in the garage. Two food trucks were parked at the side entrance to the property. A bale of hay had been set there in case the dirt turned muddy. Well, the hay just mixed in with the dirt, and it was just a muddy expanse. The rain stopped again, and guests made their way to the food truck in spite of the mud. Everyone was having a great time despite the weather. The bride and bridesmaids had discarded their shoes, pulled up their dresses, and carried on. There were lots of pictures of the bride and bridesmaids with muddy feet and muddy dress hems and big smiles on their faces. The cake was cut under the DJ's tent with toasts from friends and family while a light rain fell. The rain stopped at the end of the evening as everyone gathered around the pool to light candles to remember the bride's deceased mother and to make wishes for the new couple. The many friends of the bride and groom were reported as saying it was the best wedding they'd ever been to. It was a happening. With all the rain and mud, I called this the "Woodstock Wedding," thus harking back to that event in upstate New York where everyone came together in the rain and the mud and had a joyous time!

1) The back of the property and pool all set for the reception. 2) The beautiful ceremony went off without a hitch, 3) We were soaking wet in the downpour, covering all the furniture with plastic.

Everything is an Event

The intention for this wedding was to bring family and friends together in joyful celebration. It was filled with lots of heart and love, and it turned out that it didn't matter that the rain poured and the water gushed. The guests partied till the end as one community supporting the bride and groom. The evening was filled with laughter, fun, and merriment. Everyone went with the flow—literally and figuratively—and had a wonderful time doing so. This was a superb example that you plan for all the contingencies and details that you can. Yes, we had a huge roll of plastic to cover the wooden pews and furniture. And the weather was in charge. What could have seemed like a disaster wasn't at all. I moved the event timeline along as best as possible; when the rain stopped, they got in the first dance. Food was served, and when it was time for cake and toasts, the little light rain was ignored. The end of the evening with no more rain was a very special and moving ceremony with everyone gathered around the pool, speaking their wishes for the couple and their remembrances of the bride's mother. It reminds me of my mantra, it's all unfolding perfectly. Whatever happens is perfect just the way it is. The way it is IS perfect. The guests' rave reviews about being the best wedding they'd ever been to reflect this. It certainly was the most memorable!

1) Hallie, the happy bride, dancing in the light rain, 2) food trucks, 3) Bride and one of the bridesmaids with shoes off, muddy feet and have a great time, 4) Bride and Groom, Hallie and Adam, at the pool in the rain, 5) the rain stopped to allow a heartfelt ceremony around the pool to honor the brides' deceased mother.

I WILL ARRIVE AT THE PERFECT TIME

Decades ago, when I started working for Martha Stewart as the executive director of her catering business, I would rush out of the office, and while driving to an appointment with a client, I would be saying to myself over and over, "I'm going to be late." I finally decided this was a terrible way to arrive at an appointment. So, I started to practice repeating, "I will arrive at the perfect time." Invariably, it would turn out to be true. I could arrive ten minutes late according to the clock and the appointment time, but it would be exactly the same time as when the client arrived. Plus, this proved to be a much calmer way to arrive at my appointment. Try it and see what happens!

Again, as I mentioned above, I'm not talking about perfection. Obviously, arriving ten minutes later than the scheduled appointment would not be perfect. But it's the perfect time—arriving at the same time as the client. This thought process relieves me from the expectation of perfection and changes my mood to one of expectation for the meeting rather than nagging myself about being wrong or being late. You could call it arriving at the right time. It's perfect whatever it is!

LET THE BROWNIES COOL

This is an important reminder when writing copy for letters, signs, invitations, email blasts, press releases, programs, and more. Don't just push the send button. Brownies are too hot to eat just out of the oven. You have to let them cool, at least a little, before sampling a piece. Get up from your desk, go do something else, and then come back to look again at what you have written with fresh eyes. Have someone else proofread it, too. New eyes can catch something you may have skipped over repeatedly. Also, print out your materials. Don't just read it on your computer. I have caught many things on paper that I didn't see on the screen. It also helps me look at the whole message to ensure it is clear and all pertinent information is included. Do I have the date, time (beginning and end), place/address, directions, and any other important info? Phone number and email address? You want to get this right the first time so you don't have to send follow-up information that you forgot to include.

A friend shared with me that she knew that the following Saturday was her daughter's school gala, however, it wasn't until four days before the event that the school posted the time. That would seem to me to be an important detail that would be

Everything is an Event

nice to know sooner than four days before the event. Be kind and communicate ALL the pertinent details so that your guests can plan ahead!

WHOEVER SHOWS UP ARE THE RIGHT PEOPLE

I have seen this proven time and time again. With large nonprofit galas, there have been instances when fewer people attend the event than the previous year. The committee for a large nonprofit gala was very concerned that they had about 600 guests attending—about 100 less than the previous year. Actually, it turned out they raised MORE money than the previous year.

The committee for a sustainability conference clarified and defined whom they wanted to attend. They had 150 people instead of 200 that year, and they were the RIGHT people who could take the conference message out into the community. This also applies to your own dinner party or child's birthday party. Many times, not everyone who says they are coming will show up. You want to party with all the guests that are present and not focus on those who did not attend.

THERE IS NO UNIMPORTANT PERSON—OR PART—TO THE WHOLE

This mantra requires practicing holistic thinking—thinking about the macro, the big picture of the event. I found that if I held this mantra as an intention, it manifested as greater community and connection between staff, vendors, and guests. No matter how "small" a job is that needs to get done for an event, it contributes to the success of the whole. Everyone has an important role to play. What is also important about this concept is to acknowledge each person's contribution, no matter the size. This builds a greater energy of connection for all involved.

I planned and coordinated a large annual event with three days of evening receptions and thousands in attendance. I had a management staff of twelve and over 100 volunteers. My intention was to let all the staff know they were appreciated and to communicate that every job was important. I communicated this individually and collectively. Also included in this intention were the restaurants and the chefs and their staff that participated in the event. One chef said he had never worked an event where he felt so appreciated and taken care of. My staff worked like crazy and kept coming back the next year to do it again. We had fun, we worked hard, and they all knew I appreciated everything they did. I watched this positive attitude spread throughout the event.

You could call this hospitality. New York restaurateur Danny Meyer (creator of Union Square Café and Shake Shack) defines hospitality as the "degree to which it makes you feel good to make other people feel good." Someone who has a high Hospitality Quotient (or HQ) is at their best when providing happiness to someone else. Seems to me like that's the event planner or host's job.

There are many ways to acknowledge guests and provide hospitality. An afternoon reception that I coordinated for about twenty-four guests in a client's home featured a talk by a well-known author. The client took photos of each guest with the author after they had a book personally signed. I received an email the next day from my client with a photo of me with the author. It was a very personal way to acknowledge a special afternoon. I know they sent a photo to each of their guests. That reminded me of my daughter's birthday parties when she was young. I decorated two children's chairs with fancy tall, gold (foam core) backs. The birthday girl sat in one chair, and the friend, whose gift was being opened, sat in the other. This gave me the opportunity to take a picture of each girl when her gift was being opened. The photo was then enclosed with a mailed thank you note. Thoughtfulness—it shows in the details, and it's the details that others remember.

MINE YOUR WEALTH

We are always sitting in the middle of resources we already have. We have connections and people we know. If we can start by remembering this, we can mine the wealth we already have. Whatever we need, we have the resources and the connections to start the ball rolling. Just start where you are. Who do I know? Who can I call? Who do they know? One thing leads to another. For organizations and nonprofits, this is an important fact that is so many times overlooked.

I worked with a nonprofit that had not really reached out to all the potential sponsors they needed to support their annual event. However, they didn't realize there was more that could be done. I met with the board of directors and talked to them, saying, "Who do you know? Who is someone you know you could invite to be a sponsor and would be a fit to support the organization?" Everyone has people in their network they can connect with. Also, they could ask their people whom they might know. The web of life. We are all connected. Not surprisingly sponsorships began to increase that year. Remember also, **what you focus on increases.**

Even with home entertaining, you can mine your wealth. Reach out to friends and associates if you have questions or don't know the right resource for something. People are always willing to help. As an event professional, I have never felt I needed to know everything. My job was knowing who to contact to start finding the answer.

SHOP AT HOME

This is a personal motto of mine, and because I have said it so many times—that makes it a mantra! I should probably explain that my first career was fashion retailing and buying, so I became an expert at comparison shopping—shopping other stores to see what they were featuring. So, I shop everywhere. On the beach, I shop for shells or rocks. I have a rock that looks like a shoe and several that are heart-shaped. I shop when I take a hike or a walk in the woods. It may be just a leaf or a twig that looks like a female figure. Shopping—it's a practice.

If I am looking for something that I want or need, I start by shopping at home. I probably already have it or have something I can use. If I am rearranging furniture and I need something for a particular spot, I shop at home. Eventually, I will find something that works. I like to discover new and different ways to repurpose furniture and accessories. Just by repeating this mantra, I know that I will find things at home I didn't think about using in a new way.

How does this apply to events? For example, if you are hosting a party in your home, you will perhaps need to look at how to open up your space to accommodate your guests and to create greater ease and flow. Maybe you need a place for your beverages. Shop at home! Repurpose what you already have. Cover it with a linen tablecloth and it will look totally different. Be open! If you have an event space you need to use, look at it with new eyes and see what you can discover to transform the space with what is already there.

Yes, I shopped and found this rock that looks like a shoe while walking along a rocky riverbed.

When the weather changed the plans for the memorial, I was helping my friend Hilda with, I shopped in the space and found tables in the back room to use for a guest book, and for displaying photos of the deceased. Scour an event space to find items you can use. There's always something. And then drape it with linen and it is transformed!

LESS WORK, MORE FUN

This started as a tagline on the label for a barbeque sauce my partner and I developed and sold years ago to Williams Sonoma and other stores. I have used it in my business ever since. I want to work less and have more fun, don't you? My personal motto is that *if you are not having fun, you are wasting time.* To work less brings up the question, "How can I do this task more easily?" This is a great lens to look through for every aspect of my life. Ease. Fun. Key qualities I want in my life. With events, they HAVE to be fun—or why would anyone want to BE THERE? **Every action you take should reflect the same intention you have for the end result.** How you do one thing is how you do everything. Let me repeat that—**how you do one thing is how you do everything**. Notice what you are thinking and what your intention is for your event. Your attitude is important.

· ·

It may seem that there are too many mantras to start using. I agree; you can't adopt all of them at once. Start with the one that seems most right for you. Practice it daily. Practice means repeating it to yourself over and over. Be open to how the mantra will show up in your experience. Be in the question; *I wonder what this will look like?* Or, *I wonder, how will this show up?* Keep up the practice and keep looking! Wonderful surprises can appear!

IT'S NOT OVER WHEN IT'S OVER

The event is over, the guests have departed, and now there is breakdown and cleanup. Depending upon the size of the event determines the number of hands required. At the end of an event, people who have been through the setup and the event are tired. It helps to have fresh hands to help with the breakdown. Especially with volunteers, breaking the jobs into smaller pieces allows others to help without having anyone feel overwhelmed. Plus, you have more people committed to the success of the event with their participation. It's a win-win.

And it's still not over! There can be follow-up for days after the event—making sure all billing is handled. Did the rentals get picked up the next day? Thank you notes to guests and/or sponsors need to be drafted, printed, and mailed. If working with a committee, schedule an event review meeting. If it's an annual event, I always schedule a meeting to review with the committee what worked, what didn't work, what to improve, and what to add for next year. I write up the notes from the meeting so there is a record to refer to as there's usually a few months' pause before starting to plan again.

And . . . after it's over, get a massage! You deserve it.

There's more that continues after an event.

REMEMBER THE PRINCIPLE,

When you have fun and create community, the buzz will follow, the memories will follow. These are by-products of the event experience.

Fun is the energy of attraction. With a celebration of life, there is perhaps not so much fun but joy—remembering with love the person who has passed. Gathering together creates connection with everyone present no matter what kind of event. The memories and buzz after an event continue for weeks, months, and even years. That's what you want to build on for an annual event as those who attended will want to be back next year and bring their friends.

The memories may also result from one-off events from weddings to milestone birthdays or anniversaries and other special occasions. Recently, a friend reminisced about the ceremony I coordinated for scattering a loved one's ashes. He said it was the sweetest and most moving experience he'd ever had, and he wants that to be what others do for him when he has passed. That ceremony was over ten years ago. As Maya Angelou said, "**people remember how you make them feel.**"

"Good order is the foundation of all good things."

–Edmund Burke

Chapter Four

How to Plan and Use the Tools

Planning is first, thinking about your event, all the different pieces and aspects, and the whole picture that you envision. You must first have the vision of the total event, what it could look like and feel like—and why you are doing the event. That's the macro—the big picture. Then start to put it all down on paper—all the parts. That's the micro—the details. All the details support the purpose, the big picture, of why you are doing the event. Remember, there is no unimportant part to the whole. In fact, people will remember the little details the most.

I start by writing down notes on paper. Yes, pen and paper. After I have reviewed the main elements of the event—see the list below—I will then put together a binder and make files on the computer that reflect the same tabs in the binder. Most of my writing is done on my laptop—making the lists, contact info, etc. that I print out and put in the binder. The binder is so you have everything in one place.

You are manifesting something physical, so you need a physical binder.

Have you started your binder yet? Now's the time. Fill in the information below or type it up on your computer so you start putting the pieces together. Then make the tabs in your binder, and folders in your computer. Do you think this sounds like more work than you want to do? What if there's a power outage or no internet access? Having it all in your binder means you have it in hand with easy access and immediately available. Trust me on this one.

Remember . . . the more planning you do ahead of time, the more at ease and relaxed you will be! By putting it all down on paper, you don't have to try and remember details—you can follow your plan. Here's a

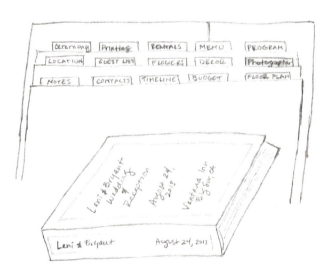

Everything is an Event 61

checklist of specifics to consider. Some will apply but maybe not all. At least this will help you get started thinking about all the aspects of your event.

1. Event date
2. Type of event
3. Event purpose
4. Location
5. Number of guests (adults and children)
6. Timing of event (when does it start and end?)
7. Invitations (save the date and invite)
8. Printed materials (what do you need? Name tags, place cards, program, signs
9. Caterer's contact info
10. Staff (for home entertaining with twenty-plus guests—get staff help!)
11. Rentals needed—tables, chairs, linen, dishes, glassware, flatware, etc.
12. Rental Company contact info
13. Décor (lighting, linens, arrangement of the space)
14. Flowers (centerpieces, potted plants at front door/entrance)
15. Music (for home entertaining, have music playing in the background)
16. Photographer
17. Valet contact info (for large parties—even at home if parking is difficult)
18. Menu (write out your menu—hors d'oeuvres, entrée, sides, and dessert)
19. Bar and beverages (include still and sparking water, remember ice)
20. Create event timeline—remember to work backward from your date to include all the actions and prep time/the number of days prior to event and for all actions that occur during event and after for breakdown

Okay . . . you looked over this list and your stomach clenched. Let's go through these items on the list one by one. It's really how you think about each detail.

FIRST THINGS TO DECIDE

1) Date

You do have to decide on a date. That's the first step. This sounds obvious but this is where people can get stuck. If you are having a hard time picking a date, can you sort through what's underneath that hesitation? Maybe you need info from someone else or there's an underlying emotional reason. Maybe you need to ask for help? Get a trusted friend or relative to discuss possible dates with you. It always helps to have someone with whom you can review ideas.

2) Type of Event

You decided on a date for your event. You then probably know what type of event it will be as that's the reason you set a date, so write down the kind of event you are hosting.

3) Purpose

Connection is always a main purpose of every event as bringing people together is what events are about. Be clear about what your purpose is. Keep the Macro always in mind. What do you want your guests to experience? What is the atmosphere you want them to walk into? Why are you hosting the event? Write it down.

4) Location

This could be your home, someone else's home, or an event space, which could be a hotel, a community center, or other event space. If it's an event space of any kind, confirm the date with the location before any other planning. It's not unusual to look at several event spaces before making a final decision. If renting a space, find out what the terms are, if insurance is required or if there are noise ordinances, the time the event must end, the setup and breakdown requirements, etc.

5) Number of Guests

First, make of list of those you want to invite. Write down the names and count. Be clear if children are invited or if it's only adults. If it's a child's birthday party, list the children invited. The number of guests will determine the location or, the location will determine the number of guests you can invite—even if it's at your house. I usually don't have more than twenty guests in my house. When I've had a crowd of forty or more for a special occasion, I plan an outdoor summer party and line up eight-foot tables up along my flowerbed wall in the backyard that's wide enough and the right height for seating. I only need to rent chairs for the other side of the rented tables. The buffet and bar on are the back deck and there are lots of places for people to gather for drinks and hors d'oeuvres before sitting down to dinner. It's a casual fun evening.

Once you've decided on the invitation list, go to the next step, and put the names on an Excel spreadsheet with their name, phone, and email with an additional column for "yes" or "no." You will fill in a number one for yes or zero for no as you hear back from responses and the spreadsheet will total the count. Make a separate list for kids, which will help with menu planning. If it's a children's party, list the parents separately so you know how many adults you are taking care of.

Be prepared to follow up on your invitations. People have lost the ability to respond to invitations. I wish I could train people to remember that when a host has taken the time to think of them and invite them, they need to reply yes or no. I wish they would understand the need for advanced notice by the host. Be courteous and respond! The host needs to plan food service for the number of guests that responded they will attend—and they really do need to know at least two weeks in advance! Since most people are not trained to reply, you will have to be prepared to call and/or email guests to confirm if they are coming or not. This applies to all kinds of events, especially more formal events such as a fiftieth or sixtieth birthday celebrations, a wedding, or milestone anniversary. I suggest that invitations don't use "please rsvp" as rsvp is French, and it seems that most people don't know French or that it means répondez s'il vous plaît. Use the English, "please respond by (date)." It's clearer.

Remember, life is always changing, so some people may cancel at the last minute. It happens. For a formal event, such as a wedding, If they cancel within the two-week window before your event, you may not be able to change the count for your caterer. Keep the communication lines open with your caterer so that they can accommodate changes wherever possible.

6) Timing of Event

When to start and when to end the party? Be clear. Guests really do want to know your plans for the party. I don't suggest leaving it open-ended. A three- to four-hour party is a nice amount of time. A cocktail party of three hours is perfect, I think. Such as inviting your guests from 5:00 to 8:00 p.m. A dinner party could go to three and a half or four hours max. A wedding with a ceremony is usually about five to six hours at the most. For many weddings, there may be an "after-party" at another location after the wedding and reception. That time is not part of the main event.

NEXT DECISIONS TO BE MADE

7) Invitations

Yes, I know a lot of invitations are sent via evite. However, I suggest using the U.S. Postal Service and mail invitations. They will get noticed way more than evite as emails can be missed. A mailed invitation also indicates that you are planning something special and have thought about who is important enough to be part of that celebration. All events don't require formal invitations. There are all kinds of fun and humorous ways to invite your guests and send a message that this will be an event they won't want to miss. Emails are fine for further communication and follow-up on your invitation.

If it's a child's birthday or a dinner party, send out invitations four to six weeks in advance. You need to give guests even more advanced notice for a wedding, major birthday, or anniversary bash. You are probably inviting friends and family that you want to be present, so give them enough notice to get it on their calendars. You will already be starting to plan these so let them know. Six months prior to the date, send out a Save the Date with more information to be sent in the next month or two. If it's a wedding that everyone is gathering at an out-of-town location, six months is not too soon to let everyone know all the details with the Save the Date sent prior to sending all the info. Because wedding locations and caterers get booked up, it is not unusual to require booking a wedding date, location, and caterer a year in advance. Nonprofit galas and conferences also need time for planning—nine to ten months usually. I suggest that if these are annual events, the date for the next year is confirmed before the gala or conference so that the next year's date can be promoted at the event.

What does a save-the-date card say? Here's an example sent six months in advance:

Save the Date
Saturday, June 13th, 2020
50th Wedding Anniversary Celebration
More information to follow

You will send a follow-up invitation a couple of months later with more details, including the location, the timing of the event, suggested dress, and other special instructions. Give your guests the gift of certainty. Let them know the who, what, where, when, why, and how. Include if valet parking is provided or other pertinent info.

Everything is an Event

If it seems that it's already too late—you've procrastinated to the eleventh hour—there is hope! Last-minute plans inviting neighbors or friends are always wonderful. I love last-minute dinner parties. No invitations needed—just call! I've called neighbors to come for dinner with a week's notice or even just a couple of days. I was gifted some freshly caught tuna one morning. I texted a few of my neighbors and invited them to come for dinner the next night—very impromptu. They were free, and we had a delicious dinner. The tuna was amazing, especially with the sauce I made for it.

The process is always the same; you start with your intention for why you are inviting your guests and how you want them to feel. If you are excited about having them come to your home, they will also be excited and anticipating a wonderful, fun time. Write it all down—who's coming, your guest count, what you will serve, and any table setting or room arrangements to be made. You then don't have to wonder if you are forgetting something. You've got a document to refer to.

If I am entertaining at home, I plan menus that are easy, meaning foods I can prepare in advance with little last-minute fixing. See #17 for more about planning menus.

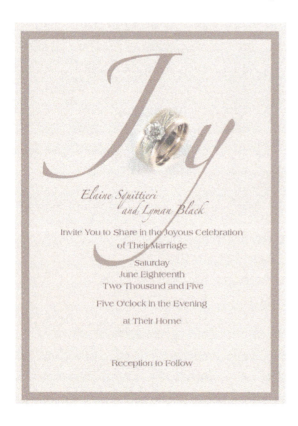

Sample wedding invitation

Even if you use evite to invite your guests, you still need a list to check off who says yes and no. Texts can be used for individual follow-up, but I don't recommend using them as a way to invite—unless it's just a few close friends. I think Paperless Post is a nicer way to email an invitation. I used Paperless Post for a virtual celebration of life invitation, and it worked very well.

Sample wedding invitation with additional cards included with the mailed invitation

8) Printed Materials

This includes invitations, save-the-date cards, place cards, escort cards (tent cards that have each guest's name on them; inside is their table name or number), programs, table number or table name cards, name tags, and signs. Consistent graphics are important to use throughout all printed materials as they tie the event together visually.

9) Caterer's Contact Info:

If you need a caterer, here's where you put in their contact information. If you have not used a caterer before, get a referral or two from people you know. Get two or three estimates before making your decision. Many food shops and restaurants also cater. They can also deliver the food and you take care of the rest. The important thing to remember about hiring a catering company is that 50% of the cost is the food and the other 50% is staff. Don't shortchange the staff as they make the difference in having unobtrusive service. Not enough staff means that dishes pile up rather than being removed so no one notices that everything is continually picked up and kept clean.

Another popular way to feed guests at weddings or other celebrations is to provide food trucks. This is fun, casual, and provides guests with several options allowing them to choose what they want to eat.

Everything is an Event

10) Staff

My rule of thumb for home entertaining is if I have more than 20 guests, I get staff to help. I want to enjoy my guests, not spend all the time serving and cleaning up. There are services that provide staff to hire if that is all you need. Don't try and do it all yourself. Sometimes you can hire high school students to help serve. Do NOT have them help with a bar as they are underage.

TIMING. Whether you have a caterer provide food and service staff, have the food delivered and hire staff, or cook the food yourself and get the teenagers in the neighborhood to help serve, plan for them to arrive two hours before your event start time. This allows for you to review the setup with the caterer or the staff. This may sound like a lot of time, but believe me, it zooms by in no time. I would rather have everything ready and have time to sit down and relax before the guests arrive instead of dashing about right up until the doorbell rings.

I consulted with a client planning a family memorial gathering in her home and needed staff. I helped her get the staff she needed. The client thought the staff should arrive at the same time as the guests. I explained that she needed time to show the staff everything that was planned and review what food had been ordered to be delivered and how it was to be served before anyone was around—and the staff should arrive two hours prior to her guests. It made all the difference in providing a gathering with ease for the client.

11) Rentals Needed

Rental Company Contact Info:

Sometimes you need to rent tables, chairs, and linen. Other times you may need to rent more such as dishes, glassware, and flatware. This will depend on the size of the event you are hosting and the location. If you are using an event space, they may have tables and chairs. Some places also have dishes. If you use their dishes, they have to be washed and put away afterward—so keep that in mind. Rental companies provide lots of choices of linen tablecloths and napkins. Putting tablecloths on tables is an instant way to dress up a space.

12) Décor

For me, décor is the big picture of the event space. How will it look and feel? Can the space be arranged so that it is inviting and there is ease of flow through the space? Choosing colored tablecloths on the tables starts the décor. **Use just one color of linen for a harmonious look.** This provides ease for the eye and ties the space together.

Lighting is also a very cost-effective way to decorate. Lighting creates an ambiance and is also functional, lighting up dark spaces so guests can move safely through the space. There are lots of different effects you can get from strings of white Christmas lights, uplights that wash wall areas with soft ambient light, or spotlights and decorative globe lights. Be mindful that you may need to provide lighting for paths or other areas for the safety of the guests.

13) Flowers

Fresh flowers do make a difference. Even simple centerpieces on tables make an impact. If there are a lot of tables for your event, remember that just a simple centerpiece repeated on all the tables creates a great impression. When you multiply the same décor element such as centerpieces, the overall effect has a big impact. Potted plants are a cost-effective way to add centerpieces to tables as well as placed at the entrance to the event or even at your front door.

The RULE for centerpieces is to NOT have centerpieces any taller than twelve inches.

Otherwise, the guests will remove them so they can see across the table and converse with their tablemates. I've watched this happen too many times with centerpieces put on the floor and out of the way. Remember, your event is about creating connection among the guests you invite. You want every detail to support building community.

All flowers are now seeming to get their due, including weeds and other wildflowers. Seed heads and branches of leaves can be interspersed with more commonly recognized flowers. Just like in fashion, there are no rules—you can always mix flowers with an eye toward harmony and beauty.

Unless you have a florist in your family, I recommend finding a professional florist to make bridal bouquets and boutonnieres. They don't have to be elaborate, however, there is an art to creating bouquets. When my niece got married, she had the florist make a bouquet of fresh herbs rather than flowers and a wreath of leaves to wear in her hair. It was perfect for her country wedding and looked wonderful with her simple and elegant white wedding dress.

14) Music

Music sets a mood. It's the unseen ingredient that creates a more welcoming atmosphere in the space when guests arrive. Live music has more energy, I believe, and adds extra vibrancy to the space. However, recorded music is also fine. When I entertain at home, I always have music playing in the background. DJs are another choice to provide the music for a party. It's your party, you decide what kind of music you want. Remember, music sets a mood. When guests arrive and during cocktails and hors d'oeuvres, you want upbeat but soft music so guests can talk and connect with each other. Softer music also applies to dinner with guests sitting around the table. They're not going to enjoy having to scream at each other. Loud music will have them walking out the door—or leaving the area. I've watched this happen. When it's time to dance, then crank up the beat that invites everyone onto the dance floor.

15) Photographer

Yes, everyone can take photos with their phones. There are events, such as weddings or other more formal events, where you may want to consider having a professional on board. It really does make a difference. Get two to three estimates before deciding on the photographer. It's a matter of cost and finding the right relationship with the photographer. Both are important.

Please note: in planning ahead for a wedding, make a list of photos you want captured by the photographer. Enlist a family member or close friend who knows your family to coordinate the list with the photographer. They will know your family members and can gather them as needed. The photographer does not know who's who in your family.

Yes, you can have your guests take photos and post them to the site you provide. Providing a backdrop that is set up for guests to take photos of their friends is a wonderful way to encourage your guests to take photos to post on Instagram or on your site.

16) Valet contact info

Having valet service is about taking care of your guests. At an event location where parking is difficult, valet is a good idea. If you are hosting a large party in your home and parking is not easy, take care of your guests and book the valet. Your guests will so appreciate it. It's also a welcomed service with a corporate or nonprofit gala.

17) Menu

If you work with a caterer to develop a menu or choose from their suggested menus, you don't need to figure out how to make it all happen. It's taken care of. However, if you are doing the cooking or even planning the menu for some things that will be delivered, it's important to think about the food that will be served. First, think simple and seasonal. There are so many resources from online sites such as the *New York Times*, *Epicurious*, and others—and, of course, wonderful cookbooks. I like to search online and in my cookbooks for inspiration and ideas—always with an eye toward what's fresh in season at the farmers' market.

Have some nibbles when guests arrive to enjoy with a beverage. Put out hors d'oeuvres that cover everyone's food choices from vegetarian to gluten-free, such as crudité—raw and blanched vegetables—with hummus and other dips, some cheeses, crackers, and maybe one more item. (Note: raw broccoli and cauliflower are not enticing or easy to eat. They are much better after you blanch them—cooked in boiling water for a minute or two, then removed and chilled in ice water—they should be crunchy but not raw. Their color is also brighter when you blanch them.) Your preparation of the food as well as the space says you have thought about taking care of your guests.

If you are making the food, figure out your menu and write it all down. Plan to have an entrée that can be done ahead of time or pulled out of the oven just before you are ready to serve the dinner buffet. A baked side of salmon with a sauce verte (green sauce) is easy and great for summer and can be served at room temperature with some salads such as a mixed green salad, a vegetable salad, and a quinoa salad. Or you could grill chicken and vegetables. All can be done in advance of your party time, so you are done cooking and the buffet is set. In winter, I have made a variety of chicken dishes that are baked in the oven. Again, provide several vegetable dishes and a mixed green salad. Have the salad prepped in the fridge and toss it with the vinaigrette just before serving. I always want to make sure my menu accommodates all my guests, whatever their food preferences.

See some menu suggestions in the Appendix.

18) Bar/beverages

Beverages are part of the menu, but it's good to address them separately. You want to make sure you are taking care of everyone that attends. Have non-alcoholic beverages plus wine and beer. It's not necessary to provide a full bar unless that is what your crowd prefers. For most events that I do, the beverages include sparkling mineral water, still water, red and white wine, sparkling wine or champagne, and iced tea, shrubs, or some other interesting non-alcoholic beverage. If children are included, make sure you have lemonade or something else that is appropriate for them.

Remember ICE for your beverages. For a large party, you may need to rent some ice tubs if you don't have them. It's not necessary to refrigerate the bottles of wine and other beverages in advance. Put the bottles in the ice tub and then pour the ice over them. All will be chilled and ready in one hour.

19) Create an event timeline

One of the most important tools to create order and give you peace of mind is an event timeline. This document lists everything that happens from the beginning of setup through all aspects of your event to breakdown and cleanup. When you have collected all the parts of your event together in your binder and have confirmed all contracts, timing, and details, and it's getting close to your event—whether it's a couple weeks or a couple of months in advance, it's time to start creating your event timeline. This is not a one-time job. I review and adjust the timeline over and over, week after week. As I make calls to reconfirm the delivery and arrival times of vendors, I make further adjustments to the timeline. Remember, follow-up is crucial.

The event timeline pulls together all the event elements and puts it all down on paper—exactly when each item is occurring. See samples in Appendix B at the back of the book. I use an Excel spreadsheet. Yes, there is plenty of event software available, but I personally haven't found that I need something more elaborate than a spreadsheet. It's really the thinking about the event and all the pieces that by putting it all down in a sequential way helps me get a feel for the event and its flow. I start to get really excited about an event when I can **Time Travel using the event timeline**.

PRINCIPLE #13:
TIME TRAVEL: DO THE EVENT BEFORE THE EVENT

I teach my clients to **Time Travel**. When I review the event timeline, I picture the date, time, and place, and with a map or floor plan, I put myself in that place in the future. I envision walking through the space in my mind. How will the space look and feel? Could I move through the space easily if I were a guest? I review the event timeline in meetings with others who are involved in the event. Each time the event timeline is reviewed, details emerge that need to be addressed or added. That's **anticipation.** Anticipating is defined by the *Merriam-Webster Dictionary* as "to give advance thought to; to foresee and deal with in advance." Anticipating what needs to be addressed before the event allows you to take care of these things in advance so that what might occur is already handled. This leaves you free at the event to address whatever shows up in the moment.

NOTE: Time Travel and do the event before it happens over and over. It's not a one-time exercise. What do I mean by this? I review an event timeline a couple times a week—for weeks prior to the event. I also review it with others that are very involved with the event, which can be a client or a committee, for example. When I start creating the event timeline, there are missing items. Someone's cell number or a reconfirmation of a delivery time and the name of the person making the delivery. Each time I review the timeline, I find things that bring up questions or that need to be addressed. Over and over, I review the event timeline. I finally print copies the day before the event to give everyone involved a physical copy. My copy goes on the top of my clipboard to refer to throughout the event.

This always reminds me of the time I was coordinating a wedding held in a mansion on a beautiful property in Connecticut. The main room was set up for the ceremony with chairs for 100 guests facing the fireplace. At the back of the room was a staircase that the bridal party would be coming down. I went upstairs to check on the bride and bridesmaids as we were getting close to the ceremony time. They were all wearing new shoes and were concerned they would slip on the carpeted

Everything is an Event

stairs. I dashed to the kitchen where the catering staff was busy prepping the food. I rummaged through the tools and equipment and found a cheese grater. I took that back upstairs and grated the bottoms of the girls' shoes—roughing up the soles so they wouldn't slip. You never know what little detail needs to be handled on-site. If you've taken care of everything else, having done the event before the event—Time Traveling with the event timeline many times—you will have the space and time to tackle whatever else shows up.

I print out numerous copies of the event timeline and share them with everyone who needs to know what's happening at each moment. Don't rely on your phone or laptop; PRINT out copies. If there's no Wi-Fi reception at your event location, you then do not have access to your timeline and other materials. I always bring my binder to my events and put all the most important documents (rental list, staff list, map, etc.) on my clipboard with my event timeline. This is a physical event, so you need physical documents.

What is your main role at your event, having Time Traveled and "done the event before the event" many times? You are the orchestra leader, making sure every part takes care of their responsibilities. Check in, follow up, and follow up again and again! Anticipate and check in with staff, vendors, etc. prior to the time when they need to do something. An orchestra conductor knows the music by heart and knows what's coming next to be ready to give direction.

I have been consulting with a nonprofit organization on their annual gala for many years. When I started, they did not have an event timeline and had been producing the event for 20 years. The Executive Director said that having the event timeline gave her a clear plan for where and when she was to be doing different things and she now had certainty and clarity. It provided greater ease for her to know what to expect as the event preceded and made a huge difference in her ability to relax and be present.

That's the point of planning ahead.

A BIG SUR WEDDING

Sometimes planning ahead doesn't actually cover everything that needs to be addressed. I ran into my friend, Leni, in June. She introduced me to her fiancé, Bryant, and said they were getting married in Big Sur in August. I had coordinated Leni's daughter's wedding almost 20 years before. "How are the wedding plans coming along?" I asked. "What plans?" asked Leni. "Maybe I need to schedule a consultation with you soon," she said. Leni explained that she and Bryant had met on OK Cupid. She was not looking for a relationship—she was interested in looking at their analytics for her business, but to do so, she had to sign up. She got an email from a man, and she told him she wouldn't meet with him but would agree to emails. They emailed back and forth for over a month and then finally agreed to meet. Both Leni and Bryant said they wouldn't have connected like they did if they hadn't had the time just to email. Two years later they were planning on getting married.

When we met, I learned that Leni and Bryant had reserved the Ventana Inn in Big Sur for the wedding and had reserved rooms at a couple of nearby places for their friends to stay for the weekend. There would be about fifty family and friends attending. Turns out those were all the plans that had been made. No rehearsal dinner Friday night, no menu planned for the wedding, no flowers, no music, and many other details had not been addressed. I had lots of questions starting with "What is the experience you want for yourselves and for your guests? What are the qualities you want to experience?" I explained that this is an especially important question to ask when planning a wedding, as it is the foundation for all the details that are planned. Leni was floored that I asked this question—something she had not ever thought about.

About thirty minutes into our meeting, Leni said, "We need to hire you!" We discussed their ideas for their wedding weekend, and I wrote down the list of the qualities as they named them: celebration, community, family, connection, peace, harmony, beauty, openness, ease, casual, elegant, accessible, surprise, fun, joy, gratitude, blessed, oneness, humor, and inspiration. Then we started exploring what would fulfill those qualities. It was really important that their friends coming from across the country would get to know each other.

I got busy putting all the pieces together with just two months to make this happen. With a weekend event, activities and plans for gathering with the guests and celebrations required detailed planning for the three days. I started filling in an **event timeline** to see what all was needed. I put those qualities that they wanted to the experience at the top of the event timeline.

I researched florists in the Big Sur area as well as musicians for the wedding ceremony and a DJ for the dinner. To keep costs down, I found a Mexican restaurant that was able to provide the food for a buffet for the Friday dinner, so a colorful

Mexican theme became the look for the printed elements and decor. Leni and Bryant wanted a videographer, so that was another search. Collecting all the pieces was like pulling all the threads to create a tapestry for the weekend of events. I created a list of all the contacts, saved the document on my computer, printed it out, and put it in my binder.

As all guests were coming from out of town, we wanted to make sure all felt welcome and appreciated, so a program was needed to list what was happening when during the weekend. It's always good to provide clarity, and it gives the guests the gift of certainty so they know when and where they need to be over the weekend. Leni and I started putting together items for gift bags for each of the guests to be handed out after the Friday dinner.

I confirmed the use of the meeting space at Big Sur Lodge, where many guests were staying for the Friday dinner, and planned the layout of the room with round dinner tables and rectangular tables for hors d'oeuvres and check-in. In many conversations with my contact at Ventana Inn, we finalized plans for the ceremony space, the reception and dinner, the dinner table layout, and the Sunday morning brunch. I created floor plans with my CAD program and printed them out. Bryant took the lead in creating the seating arrangements for both the Friday and Saturday dinners—using my Post-it seating method.

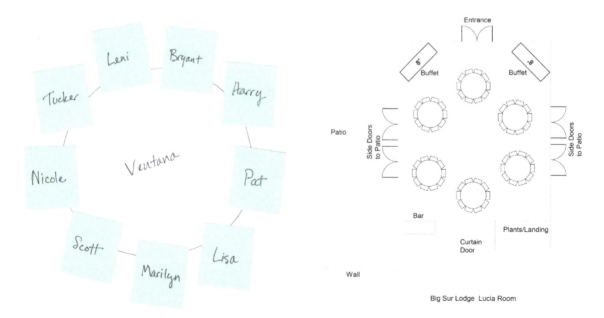

Sample of post it seating chart for one table and the floorplan I created for the room set up.

76 *Everything is an Event*

How To Do Seating with the Post-it Method:

Yes, you can use a spreadsheet, but really that's after you do this. I have used this method with many clients over many years, and it is the easiest way to arrange seating. Really!

1) Draw circles or rectangles—one each on a sheet of paper. Use small Post-its with each guest's name written on one.

Marinda & Bryant doing Post It seating charts.

2) Move the "people" around on each page/table to see what will work best and connect people in an interesting and fun way. Perhaps mix people with those they don't know. Be strategic and think about how you can introduce your guests to each other or who needs to sit with each other.

3) Print a list of guests at each table for easy reference. It's also good to photocopy the pages with the Post-its so you have copies of all the tables but not the originals where the Post-its can fall off.

Reviewing the **floor plans** I created showing the layout of tables for each evening, Leni and Bryant named all the tables. Once all the seating arrangements were finalized, I put the guest names and tables on an Excel spreadsheet—one tab for each dinner, so I had a printed document to refer to on-site to set out the place cards. My spreadsheet had columns as shown below. There were six tables for Friday and eight tables for Saturday.

First Name	Last Name	#	Table Name	# at Table
Leni	M	1	Ventana	9
Bryant	W	1	Ventana	
Harry	W & Pat M	2	Ventana	
Lisa	W	1	Ventana	
Marilyn & Scott	H	2	Ventana	
Tucker	W & Nicole O	2	Ventana	

Here's a sample of the Excel spreadsheet for Friday, showing one table. My spreadsheet continued to list each table and the guests (all listed in order of how they are seated around the table).

Everything is an Event 77

I had several phone meetings with the florist reviewing the flowers needed, and when and where they need to be delivered. Floral centerpieces for both the Friday and Saturday dinners. Bridal bouquet, corsages, and boutonnieres. There were phone calls and emails with all the vendors to review the timing of arrival for setup, timing of the program for the evening, and when the event was ending for breakdown. Communication is key to make sure everyone is on the same page. I emailed the event timeline to all the vendors so they had all the information in one place.

A month before the wedding, the bride decided that she couldn't wear the royal blue cocktail dress she bought. She needed something more appropriate for a wedding. So, I made an appointment for her with a local dressmaker that I knew from other weddings I had coordinated. Within an hour, the designer and Leni had picked out a top, skirt, and sheer jacket in a beautiful coral. In two weeks, she had the perfect ensemble made just for her.

All aspects of the ceremony had to be worked out before the **program** for the ceremony could be designed and printed—more printed material. This was completed several weeks prior to the wedding at a meeting with Leni and Bryant. The bride and groom had requested an altar for the ceremony, so I ordered a six-foot table to be rented. It was to be covered with gold fabric I would bring plus candles, incense, and other special items they provided. Oh, and then Leni called me and asked to hang a Tibetan Thangka, a sacred painting, above the altar. The ceremony is on the outdoor terrace facing the ocean. Hang it in the air?! There was nothing to hang it on! Wow, a challenge. I ended up finding a gold easel from a vendor.

Since all the guests had already been invited and confirmed, it was only necessary to send them emails with instructions about where they were staying and the timing for meeting at the dinner on Friday.

Friday morning, I packed up the royal blue linen for Friday's dinner tables (picked up at the rental company Thursday morning), name tags, escort cards, place cards, table name cards, programs, goody bag items, straight pins, my kit (see page 83 in this chapter), the gold easel, plus the items from Leni for the altar, two baskets for flower girls, pinatas, and a blindfold. I drove down to Big Sur, arriving at the Big Sur Lodge meeting room at 1:00 p.m. I started unloading all that was needed for the Friday dinner, placing the royal blue linen on the tables, and setting out the name tags and escort cards on the table outside the room. At 2:00 p.m., the florist delivered the zinnia centerpieces. I then added the table names on floral card holders set into the centerpieces and set out the place cards at each table.

I had help stringing up the pinatas and placed the blindfold nearby. All these times and actions were listed on my event timeline. Way better than trying to remember all the details, plus everyone else involved needs to know, too.

Colorful name tags in plastic sleeves with magnets (not pins, so as not to ruin anyone's clothing), designed and printed by my graphic designer, were set out on a table by the entrance with escort cards clipped to two Mexican hats with small clothespins. What are escort cards, you may ask? They are cards with the guest's name on the front and the table name or number on the back so they know what table they are sitting at. Place cards are small tent cards with the guest's name on them noting their place at their table.

At 4:00 p.m., I was at Ventana Inn for the rehearsal on the lower terrace where the ceremony would take place. All the final details for the ceremony were reviewed and confirmed with the honored Buddhist teacher, Orgyen Chowang Rinpoche, Leni, and Bryant.

The guests arrived Friday afternoon and arrived on time at 6:00 p.m. for the dinner party. It wasn't really a rehearsal dinner; it was a gathering. Glasses of wine and mineral water were passed around as the guests arrived, and they helped themselves to the hors d'oeuvres set out on a table. At 7:00 p.m., I invited guests to be seated for dinner. Leni and Bryant took turns introducing their friends and family at each of the tables and then guests were invited to the dinner buffet.

As guests departed, I handed out gift bags to each guest that included a map, a schedule of the weekend, some truffles and other goodies, and a flashlight since most were staying in nearby cabins in the woods with not much outdoor light. It is important to think ahead to what might be needed to make it easy for the guests. Flowers from the centerpieces were also handed out to the guests. I had to return the vases to the florist the next day at Ventana Inn. All the blue tablecloths were folded and put in my car to return to the rental company after the weekend.

It was a beautiful sunny day for the wedding—a perfect spot on the deck with

Everything is an Event 79

an infinite view of the ocean. I arrived at 2:00 p.m. to meet the florist—with wedding flowers and floral arrangements. Also arriving was the DJ, who set up the sound for the ceremony. Remember, sound doesn't carry well outside, so you need a microphone that allows everyone to hear the ceremony. I set up the altar with the gold tablecloth, two large flower arrangements, candles, and incense—plus my easel behind the table with the Tibetan Thangka. Once the Thangka was "hung," you couldn't see the easel. Magic! Fifty chairs were set up with a center aisle, and I put reserved signs on the chairs in front for family members. I arranged for two armless chairs for the musicians, who arrived at 3:30 p.m.—both harpists and one also played the flute. The DJ then set up for the dinner. At 4:00 p.m., the photographer and videographer arrived, and the tables for the reception were finished being set so the centerpieces could be added, plus table names and place cards. On a table near the entrance to the dinner tables, I placed a driftwood branch with the escort cards attached with small clothespins.

At 4:30 p.m., the musicians began to play, and guests began to arrive. At 5:00 p.m., with all the guests seated, the honored Buddhist teacher, Orgyen Chowang Rinpoche, was front and center and married the bride and groom in a lovely ceremony.

As guests entered the reception area, I positioned myself at the table with the escort cards, to make sure all the guests picked up their cards to know where they were seated. The musicians with harps and flute moved to the reception area to play. Waiters greeted the guests with trays

1) The ceremony area set up looking out at the Pacific Ocean, 2) Leni and Bryant in front of the altar with the Tibetan Thangka "hung" on the gold easel, 3) Escort cards clipped to a driftwood branch with small clothespins at the entrance to the Reception and Dinner area, 4) A dinner table setting with the name of the table displayed.

of wine and mineral water and hors d'oeuvres were passed. After an hour, guests were invited to a fabulous buffet dinner. There were dance sets, toasts, and cake, followed by more dancing with great music from the **DJ**. It was an elegant, joyful, and relaxed affair.

As I say it's never over then it's over. At the end of the evening, I met with the florist to return all the centerpiece vases and votive candle holders.

At brunch on Sunday, the guests were exclaiming that it felt like they'd spent the weekend with family. Some were busy making plans to meet again together with Leni and Bryant. Everyone kept repeating that it was such a beautiful and memorable wedding. Look again at the qualities that Leni and Bryant wanted for their wedding—those were what the guests expressed. Definitely a manifestation of the bride and groom's **clarity of intention** for the experience they wanted their guests to have!

When Leni, Bryant and I met for the first time, they had the question, Why do we need a wedding planner? They both said they never knew how many details there were to be addressed to create their wedding weekend and couldn't have done it without my help. They are still saying this ten years later! Because of all the detailed planning I provided, they had a weekend where they could enjoy spending time with their friends and family and know that all details were taken care of by me—the event expert!

. . . .

What happens when there are breakdowns at an event? I planned and coordinated a daylong conference for an organization with a series of panels and individual speakers. When the second group of speakers had not shown up thirty minutes prior to their scheduled speaking time, I was in the lobby calling those speakers. As I put everything on the event timeline, I had their phone numbers. Thankfully, they were all on their way and made it in time for their session. You never know who or what might not show up and you may need to follow up with a speaker, a vendor, staff, or a volunteer. Put all the contact information on the timeline and you don't have to go looking for it.

A good friend of mine hosted a sixtieth birthday celebration for his partner with about sixty guests. For the evening event, he had a tent beautifully decorated with floral centerpieces and a fabulous swing band to entertain the guests. The caterer had had an accident the day of the event, and things were a bit chaotic in the

Everything is an Event

kitchen. They seemed a bit overwhelmed and were behind in getting the dinner out to the guests. So, my friend went around to each table, pouring wine for the guests and spending some time chatting with everyone. Eventually, dinner was served. In retrospect, my friend commented that even though he was stressed out that the caterer was not serving on time, it turned out that by spending time at each table he had had a chance to visit with all the guests. The guests had no idea that there was any delay in service. That's the trick with handling on-site problems or situations. Creative problem-solving in the moment . . . see the mantra "it's all unfolding perfectly."

There's always something that will come up in the moment. That's the reason for reviewing the timeline over and over to manage all that can be handled in advance. When a surprise arises or a snafu occurs, all the advanced planning pays off. When you plan and plan, which really means reviewing all details and thinking about the event, you arrive at the event knowing exactly what will unfold, and you are free and ready to handle anything that shows up. I call that creative problem-solving on-site. I think it's fun.

When I have attended events as a guest, the last thing I want to see is a manager and/or staff running around right before an event is about to begin. To me, this means that they have not done their homework, they did not "do the event before the event" so they could anticipate any concerns or problems in advance.

Planning ahead, using the tools, and reviewing all the details over and over proves the principle—**Order Creates Greater Calm and Peace of Mind (see Principle #10 on page 25)**. It's how you handle anything in life, when you are calm you can respond, not react.

Plus . . . be prepared and bring a kit!

THE EVENT KIT TOOLBOX

I always bring my kit to every event. It's in a portable plastic toolbox I bought at the hardware store. It's filled with the tools of my event trade. Having planned and built the event, you never know what you might need on site. Here's what's in my kit:

Pens	Binder clips	String
Pencils	Paper clips	Rope
Sharpie markers	Stapler & staples	Zip ties
Highlighters	Staple remover	Wine opener
Packing tape	Hole Punch	Ruler (foldable yardstick)
Gaffers tape	Knife	Hammer
Scotch tape	Scissors (at least four)	Level
Double stick Scotch tape	Box cutters	Garbage bags
Painter's tape	Spreader	Glue stick
Duct tape	Straight pins	Rubber Bands
Wite-Out correction tape	Push pins	Band-Aids
Caution tape	Pipe & drape hooks	Business cards
Leatherman all-purpose tool	Post-its	

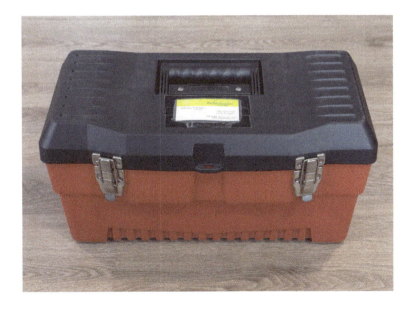

Everything is an Event 83

(above + left below) Top level of the kit contents,
(right below + bottom) Bottom level of the kit contents.

84 *Everything is an Event*

"Tomorrow belongs to those who prepare for it today."

–African Proverb

Chapter Five

Tips and Tricks, Nuts and Bolts

A toolbox includes many items you don't use every time you need the kit, but by having all the items in your toolbox, you are prepared for whatever might need fixing. For events, tools are also your knowledge of what is available so you can consider different options as you put together all the pieces that will make up your event. The following may seem like information you don't need; however, even if you are entertaining at home, these tools will help you create a harmonious, welcoming space for your guests. Here are tools and information to know—when you need it.

TABLES AND TABLECLOTHS

Linen tablecloths are an important design element for any event. One color of cloths unifies and dresses up a space. It creates a harmonizing look. Linen does not mean the fiber here, but the category of tablecloths, napkins, table runners, etc. Using linen is the simplest and most cost-effective way to pull together the look of an event.

First, it is helpful to know what sizes of tables you can rent and the sizes of linen. From there, you can determine the size of the tablecloths you need. You can also shop at discount stores for tablecloths once you know the sizes you need.

TABLES

COCKTAIL TABLES: These are thirty inches or thirty-six inches in diameter.

You can seat four to six at these tables.

All tables are thirty inches from the floor, so to cover the table with linen to the floor, you need a cloth that is ninety-inch round for the thirty-inch round table. It's thirty inches from the floor to the table, thirty inches across, and thirty inches to the floor. For the thirty-six-inch round, you add six more inches to reach the floor on both sides, which equals a 102-inch round. Many rental companies don't carry the 102-inch round, so the ninety-inch round is sufficient.

Everything is an Event

KIOSK OR STAND-UP COCKTAIL TABLES: These are thirty inches or thirty-six inches in diameter. These tables are usually bar height—forty-two inches tall—so a 120-inch round is needed to cover the table to the floor (42+42+30 = 114, or 42+42+36=120). On the thirty-inch round tables, if you have a little puddling of the linen, just kick the hems into the table so there is less chance of tripping. Another option, especially if the tables are outside, is to tie a ribbon around the linen halfway between the tabletop and the floor to keep the linen from blowing.

ROUND TABLES

For dinner tables, these range in size from forty-eight inches in diameter to seventy-two inches.

- The forty-eight-inch rounds seat six for dinner, or with not a lot of flatware and glasses set on it, it will work for eight. Cozy, but it will work.
  - 48 inches + 60 inches = 108-inch round tablecloth
- The sixty-inch rounds seat eight for dinner and can also be set for ten. The chairs need to be small enough to accommodate ten at this size table. I find this size table makes it easy for guests to talk across the table. Seating for eight gives ample room for table settings.
  - 60 inches + 60 inches = 120-inch round tablecloth
- The seventy-two-inch rounds seat twelve. The guests will definitely be seated comfortably at this size table. You have to consider the space you are setting up in and whether these large tables will work as they take up more space. This table makes it a little less easy to speak across the table because of the size, however, it seats twelve comfortably.
  - 72 inches + 60 inches = 132-inch round tablecloth
- Squeezing more to a table: depending on the chair size, it is possible to add one more to a seventy-two-inch table to squeeze in thirteen guests. For a sixty-inch round, you can squeeze one more guest for eleven at the table.

RECTANGULAR TABLES

There are four-foot, six-foot, and eight-foot tables. Standard tables for bars and buffets are the six-foot and eight-foot tables. These are all thirty inches wide and thirty inches from the floor if you get rental tables. It's always good to measure the tables you have. My forty-eight-inch round dining table is 29.5 inches to the floor. My outdoor rectangular table is 28.75 inches to the floor. Not a lot of difference in height in these tables to determine the linen that's needed.

TABLECLOTHS

Now, rental companies have cloths called drapes for the six-foot and eight-foot tables. That means that the cloths are curved at the corners, so they fit on the tables without having to box the tables (I'll explain this in a bit). You would get a six-foot or eight-foot drape for the table.

Now, I am really particular about how the linen is placed on the tables. It must be neat. On round tables, the linen needs to be even around the table to the floor. Rental linen is never exactly round; don't ask me why. Just do the best you can. And I don't want to see any table legs showing. With rectangular tables for buffets and bars, the front of the table is what is visible. Therefore, make sure the front of the linen just kisses the floor—no puddling. You don't want anyone to trip on the cloth.

If the rental company does not have drapes for your rectangular tables, then you will need to get rectangular linen. There are many sizes. It's good to know what they are so you know how flexible you can be with the linen.

SQUARE LINEN

I use these as overlays—over the tablecloth that covers the table. They can be a contrasting color from the under-cloth or just a shade different. If it's a lacey square, the main under-cloth color will dominate. It's like adding frosting to a cake.

54"x54": These squares are great as an overlay at an angle on rectangular tables or smaller rounds such as forty-eight-inch round tables.

72"x72": These squares can be overlays on sixty or seventy-two-inch rounds and at an angle on rectangular tables. To refresh a buffet that has gotten messy from service before serving dessert, bring out an overlay in the same color as the main tablecloth and lay it at an angle in a diamond shape over the table, and voila, you have a clean surface again. It's also less costly to rent the square than a whole new tablecloth to use for this purpose.

RECTANGULAR TABLECLOTHS

For rectangular tablecloths, there are many choices. The primary sizes are 90"x60", 120"x60", 144"x72", 108"x90", 132"x90", and 156"x90". Okay, don't give up on me now, even though you have to do a bit of math. If you have a six-foot-long table, you need to cover the front, both ends, and some of the back if the back is not being seen such as for a bar or buffet table. The length is figured by adding up the following: six feet is seventy-two inches plus thirty inches to the floor at each end—equals 132 inches. The width—thirty inches across the top, thirty inches to the floor in front, plus some to hang over the back. For this table, I would choose the 132"x72". If you need the table covered all the way around, the 132"x 90" would cover both the front and the back.

Both of these cloths then need to be boxed, meaning the ends need to be folded like wrapping a present.

BOXING A TABLE:

First, on a rectangular table, center the cloth so there is the same amount of fabric to the floor at each end, and make sure the front edge of the cloth is just kissing the floor. All corners of the cloth are now hanging way down on the floor. As if you were wrapping a gift or tucking in a sheet (Photo 1) take the front of the linen and wrap it around the side of the table, lining up the bottom so it's kissing the floor, and (Photo 2) smoothly tuck the top under the rest of the cloth, making the fold at the edge of the table.

1) wrap cloth around side with bottom just touching the floor, 2) smooth top of linen to edge of table, 3) boxed as seen from the front

Another way to solve the corners puddling on the floor is to tie a knot in each corner. It looks decorative and thus removes the danger of tripping.

Now that you know about the rental tables and linen sizes for tables, you can

1) Table boxed with linen on both ends, 2) What we don't want –linen on the floor, a tripping hazard, 3) A knot tied in the corner looks neat and is safe!

also figure out what size linen you would need for any table you already have. Measure from the floor to the table, the size of the tabletop—length and width or diameter—and you can determine the linen required.

SETTING THE TABLE

Setting the table is setting a mood that your guests will see when they arrive. Remember, you want your guests to feel welcome and appreciated. Setting a beautiful table will do this. Beauty creates an ambiance of ease and connection. Your guests will feel more open, at ease, relaxed, and taken care of.

I'm a stickler for perfectly set tables. I love to arrange a beautiful table. When I entertain at home, I set my table the day before so I have time to put it all together. My position is that if I set a beautiful table with flatware, napkins, glassware, and a centerpiece of flowers, fruit, or a combination of greens, I don't need to get dressed up. My table is dressed up whether it's for a celebration or just a gathering with friends. It sends a message that they matter since I took time to prepare for them. Don't forget—keep the centerpiece LOW—no higher than twelve inches. Even lower is better. You want everyone to be able to connect around the table and not be dodging a centerpiece that prevents them from seeing the person across from them!

THE BASICS:

Fork on the left—fork" has four letters and so does "left."
Knife and spoon on the right—both have five letters and so does "right."

Everything is an Event 91

If serving a salad or other first course, that fork goes on the outside of the dinner fork. When dining, you work your way through the flatware from the outside in. The spoon is always on the right of the knife. Line up the flatware straight (aligning the bottom of the flatware), like the illustration. No sloppy flatware, please! Straight means lined up vertically and horizontally all on the same line. If you are serving dessert and coffee, these are set at the top of the place setting—placed horizontally with the fork pointing right and the spoon pointing left. Got it?

Glassware is placed above the knife and spoon—edging towards the middle of the place setting with three glasses if the table is not a big one. These could be water, red and white wine glasses, or water, wine, and champagne flute.

Napkins—please use cloth napkins. This is the green alternative. They can be washed, not thrown out. Yes, paper is fine for an outdoor BBQ or other informal buffet, but not for your set table. There are many ways to arrange the napkin to the left of the fork. Folded into a rectangle or at an angle. Rolled or pulled-through a napkin ring is also nice.

Place Cards—with a dinner for six or eight, it's not necessary to have place cards. I don't if it's a more casual dinner. However, if you want to arrange the seating in a special way, it's nice to use a place card. It's another way that says you prepared for your guests' visit. There are many creative ways to create a place card. They don't always have to be tent cards. You could write each name on a leaf or cut out shapes of colored paper. Be creative. Sheets of place cards (the tent card kind) can be purchased that allow you to print the names using your computer and printer. Choose an interesting font that can be easily read, and your cards will look super professional. I've used these for client dinner parties of sixty to eighty guests.

With larger tables or seating with several tables, it is nice to give the guests direction by assigning seats with place cards. They appreciate not having to stop and figure out where to sit. Really, help them out!

For larger client affairs, weddings, rehearsal dinners, special birthdays, or anniversary celebrations, I have used a graphic designer to create a design for the place cards, the table name cards, and escort cards. It could also be used for the invitation, branding the event with a consistent look. Have I now confused you? Let me explain. If you have four or five tables or many more, it's helpful to name the tables with printed cards in the center of each table as the guests need a way to find their table. Yes, you can number them, but I find that not as interesting. For a very large wedding I coordinated, the room was divided with a dance floor in the middle. On one side of the dance floor, the dining tables had white wine names, and on the other side, the tables had red wine names, all with beautifully drawn calligraphy. For these tables of eight, place cards were used, however, you don't always have to use the place cards if you use escort cards. Escort cards are placed at a front table by the entrance to the dining room with a map of the tables and their names. (If it's just a few tables, you don't need a map as it will be easy for the guests to find their table.) The escort card has the guest's name on the front and inside or on the back is printed the name of their table. If there are no place cards, the guests can choose their seats at the table.

Here's a picture that shows a sample place setting:

This picture also shows a charger. For your really fancy dinner parties, add a charger. It's a little larger than the dinner plate. Think of it as a frame for the dinner plate, an extra layer of décor.

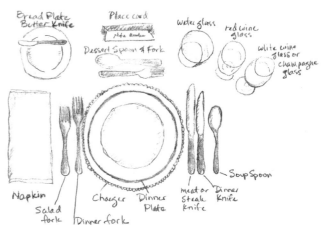

A NOTE ON CHAIRS:

Ok, you've set the table or tables with linen to the floor, table settings, napkins, flatware, glassware, and centerpieces all beautifully arranged. Now, don't ruin the picture by stuffing the chairs into the table. Chair seat fronts should be just kissing the linen, keeping the straight line of the linen to the floor. This is also important when you have a room full of dinner tables. There needs to be enough room between the tables so that when guests are seated, they can move between the tables easily. The minimum distance between tables is five feet. Six feet is even better. Remember, flow is key to allowing guests to feel comfortable moving around the space. Friends of mine attended an event and commented that the tables were way too close together, making it difficult to get through the room. They commented that if Marinda had been here, she would never have allowed the tables to be so close to each other! True. My goal is always ease!

Everything is an Event 93

When doing a large seating of ten, twenty, or fifty tables of ten, tables should be set with linen before chairs are placed at each table. I always go around and measure with my five-foot stick to make sure there is enough room between the tables. I also go around after all the tables are set to make sure the flatware is straight and glasses are placed properly, and then I place cards are put down per a map with all the names. You could call me a perfectionist. Yes, I have those tendencies, and my aim is for beauty and order. Remember, order creates greater calm and peace of mind. Beauty does the same. And . . . all the care you've taken reflects the intention of taking care of your guests.

DRAPE IT

There are other purposes for table linens such as when you need to have something go away or change the view that guests see. Drape a black tablecloth over a stack of boxes or whatever and it fades away from view. Take fabric and drape it over a wall to change what the eye sees. I used pipe and drape (pipe on bases with fabric hanging from the bar across the top connecting the two poles and bases) to cover all the walls in the entry to the community center for our school auction, thus changing the feel of the room. Visually, it creates greater calm with solid color "walls," i.e., the eye is not jumping from posters, signs, and bulletin boards posted on the walls.

I have ordered fabric from a theater resource because the fabrics come in much wider widths than in a fabric store. I've used the natural muslin I ordered to make tablecloths that I also use to drape over things that need to disappear visually in a space. For my daughter's 7th birthday, I draped the walls and ceiling of my garage in natural and pink fabrics to create a fairy tent. The girls invited were instructed to come in leotards and tights. When they arrived, they received fairy tulle skirts and wings that I made. They made fairy wands and candles, pinned the wings on the fairy, and had a *fairy* good time. When you commit to a theme, go for it.

For my daughter's fifth birthday, I draped the living room in white. I strung a sheer curtain across the width of my living room to create a smaller space (use dental floss as it won't stretch). I covered the couch and chair in white sheets and covered the floor in pastel quilts. It was a cozy space for a sleepover party for eight girls. The girls were gifted dark pink nightshirts, which were T-shirts I had decorated. My intention was to create a space that cast a sleeping spell—a calm, cozy space to encourage the girls to go to sleep as scheduled. And they did, just thirty minutes later than my party timeline. When the moms dropped off their daughters, several said they would like to hang out in the space with a glass of wine. When you start with a clear intention, you can design spaces that create a mood and an invitation.

PRINCIPLE #14:
DÉCOR—THE RULE OF THREE

Décor is the overall visual of the event space.

The rule of three. If you ever walked into a space for a dinner party and said, "Wow!", the principle is:

1. Use a single color to unify the space
2. Simple centerpieces
3. Flow of the space

You want a style of decoration that is consistent throughout the space. First and foremost, you want to create a harmonious, inviting space that guests feel good in. TAKE OUT your magic wand and manifest what you want your guests to experience. The design is generated by your intention for what you want to occur in the space and how the space visually looks and feels.

With a room of round or rectangular dinner tables, using linen to cover all the tables in the same color immediately dresses up the space and creates a mood. Whatever centerpieces you place on each table are magnified by the multiples of the same thing. Centerpieces can be flowers, but they can also be many other things, from natural leaves, gourds, fruits, and vegetables, to candles and shiny balls, and many other options. A friendly reminder again about centerpieces—they should be no higher than twelve inches. What about those tall, dramatic centerpieces, you ask? Unfortunately, I've seen them placed on the floor so many times because the guests want to be able to connect with each other around the table. Help them out!

One year, for our school auction, the theme was a '50s nightclub, like El Morocco, the Manhattan nightclub. The round dinner tables wore black and white zebra print cloths with hot pink centerpieces. It took me a while to come up with a centerpiece that was easy and very inexpensive. This was a school FUNraiser, remember?! I had many straight-sided glass bowls from a previous event that I could provide for the evening. I was after the look. Eventually, after much searching, I came across hot pink feathers. Each glass bowl was filled with feathers. Hot pink centerpieces surrounded by white votive candles on fifty black-and-white zebra print tables definitely made an impact. Simple and effective. It was also easy—the feathers were put in the bowls beforehand, and there was no water needed, so no extra mess. The cost? $1.39 per bowl of feathers.

1) The three co-chairs, 2) Table setting with pink feather centerpiece, 3) The tent filled with zebra print tablecloths and pink centerpieces and votive candles, 4) Holiday centerpiece with elegantly wrapped "gifts".

For a client holiday party, I wrapped boxes in beautiful paper, and ribbons that were used for the centerpieces. It was an appropriate look as well as cost-effective. The main cost was the paper and ribbons. A single wrapped box was on each cocktail table and several boxes of different sizes were arranged in the center of the larger round tables. The space was decorated with many Christmas trees. With the shimmering tablecloths and sparkling gift box centerpieces, everything added up to a very festive and inviting décor.

Be creative. Think outside the box of what your picture of a centerpiece is "supposed" to be. Look around. What things can you collect from nature? What about fall leaves placed with bowls of fruit? How about a bowl of sand with a single pillar candle set in the middle and some shells scattered around it for a summer party? Think seasonally. What's available now? I love potted plants because they can be used again—to be planted and grow after the event. For an annual fall lunch for a community business organization, I bought six-inch pots of cyclamen and had the hotel provide napkins that matched the tablecloths. I wrapped each pot in a napkin. (How? Take two corners on one side of the napkin, tie them together, and tuck under the leaves into the top of the pot, then do the same for the other two corners.) With fifty potted plants as centerpieces, the room always looked inviting and dressed for the occasion. At the end of the lunch, the guests were invited to take a plant—but please, leave the napkin.

Here's how to wrap a six-inch potted plant:

1) Place pot in center of tablecloth, pull the two corners together, 2) Tie the corners together and 3) Tuck into pot under the plant. 4) Turn napkin and plant around and do the same thing on this side 5) Tie the corners together and 6) Tuck into the pot under the plant. 7) Make sure the napkin is tucked into the pot all the way around. 8) Finished wrapped pot.

Pinterest, of course, is a place to see lots of ideas. Look at the pictures with an eye towards asking yourself, "What mood is being created?" What does the repetition of décor elements do to the space? It really is all about the art of display. It has to look fabulous, but it can be created out of elements that just need to hold together for one evening. Just like display windows. From the front, it looks wonderful. From the back, you might see clothespins holding the dress together so it fits the mannequin, the back of display boxes, or other elements are rough and not painted. You are

Everything is an Event 97

making vignettes—groups of décor items that dress up a space. These could be Christmas trees in groups, clusters of plants with special lighting, or other décor elements. Fluff it up. Be creative. Think differently about what is around you. Shop at home. (Remember this mantra in Chapter 3?) Shop your home or event space with new eyes, searching for ways to use furniture and other items in different ways. Rearrange the furniture to open it up and allow for ease of guests moving around the space. Look around. Repurpose tables, furniture, or whatever. Drape it and it will be transformed.

BUFFET TABLES

Many times, buffet tables are created to have different heights for platters of food. How do you do this? Plain wooden boxes, bricks, or cardboard boxes create risers of different heights. Take a linen that matches the draped buffet table and gather it around and over the risers so they "disappear." No one knows that that's what's under the trays of food; however, they see the trays at different heights, making it easy to access and see the food.

A large floral arrangement is also nice on the buffet table if it is placed at the back of the table and out of the way of the food.

LIGHTING

Lighting is another very effective way to decorate a space. It is also a cost-effective way to create a mood for a space and to make sure that certain areas are lit for safety. I have dimmer switches all over my house as it gives me to flexibility to adjust the lighting to the occasion. I can lower the light over the dinner table when we are sitting down to dinner or adjust the lighting in the living room for a warm glow.

Professionally, there are companies that provide lighting for events. There are also many things you can do on your own. White Christmas lights, called string lights, are a great way to decorate a space. They are inexpensive and are easy to put up in many different spaces. I've also used long strings of globe lights—clear ball lights to define and light a space.

Some lighting basics to know about are:

- **Uplights** shine light up the wall. These can be colored lights and create a warm mood. Peach is a warm, flattering color that people look good in.

- **Spotlights** when you need an area highlighted—literally. They are also used to light someone presenting on stage.

- **Pin spot lighting** is usually used to focus light on each dinner table. Restaurants use this lighting very often. It can also be used to highlight elements of décor.

- **Gobos** are designs or logos put over a spotlight. The light is focused on the floor of an event. When I helped coordinate our town's 100th anniversary New Year's party, an anniversary gobo was shined on the dance floor.

MUSIC

Music is part of the décor and the ambiance of the space you create. Have you ever walked into a room that had pleasant music playing? There is an aliveness and welcoming environment. Music creates a mood that the guests walk into. Of course, what kind of music playing is important. Soft background music such as jazz or other types without singing is the rule. I've used my phone or iPad with selected mellow music playing on the sound system in the space for when guests enter and during the cocktail reception. Dinner music is more of the same as you want guests to be able to chat easily. Live music is always an option and ups the energy in the space. Remember, you are creating an Energy Bubble for your guests to walk into. For an annual client holiday party in their home, a guitarist and keyboard player created a welcoming and lively mood while still playing in the background so that guests could visit and connect.

Have you ever walked into a store and been assaulted by the loud music? So loud it's hard to think to talk to your friend? This is the LAST thing you want for your event or even a party in your home. That's not the Energy Bubble you want your guests to walk into. Remember, every detail including the music is to create an atmosphere of welcome and connection.

Do you have live music or a DJ? Or both? It depends on the space and what the purpose of the event is. For weddings, many times, there is wedding ceremony music of violins and guitars, harps, or some other variation for the ceremony. These musicians will often also play during the first part of the reception while hors d'oeuvres and drinks are served, and guests can congratulate the new couple. When guests sit down to dinner, music may then be provided by a DJ or band—again, quieter music while guests eat and then move to a first dance and dancing music for everyone to join in. One of the best weddings I ever coordinated, however, the client had a different plan. They booked an amazing band with a Motown beat that got everyone up to dance between courses, and I mean everyone. You couldn't stay seated. Guests sat down for the first course. Then the band brought everyone to their feet. While all the guests were dancing, the staff cleared the first course and plated the entrée. All sat down again and then back up to dance. It was so much fun.

I recommended this format to a client regarding her daughter's wedding weekend. Together, we designed the event timeline from the rehearsal to the rehearsal dinner to the next day's wedding and reception. For the reception with a seated dinner, the plan was to get guests up and dancing between courses. This helps a seated dinner not seem so formal with guests "stuck" at their tables for a long time during the dinner service. She wasn't completely sure about the plan for the reception but was willing to go with it. After the wedding, she reported back that having people up dancing between courses created a fun and energetic reception that guests were raving about. It was also a wonderful way to connect the guests with each other and the bridal party. The opposite of a staid seated dinner.

AV—AUDIO VISUAL

For larger events, you may need sound—a microphone and speakers. This could be for announcements, a presentation, a speaker, or a program with several people speaking. There are event spaces that have a sound system. It is important to test the system out and have someone on hand that can adjust the sound. Some people speak softly, so the volume needs to be turned up—or down if they speak more loudly. If you will be showing a video or slides, you will need to rent a projector and screen. I find using a local AV company allows you to get the right equipment set up properly. They can provide a staff person to manage the system during your event, which is great insurance having a professional take care of this.

A NOTE ABOUT OUTSIDE EVENTS

Sound does not travel well outside. This is a fact. For outdoor weddings, I have provided a microphone on a stand or a wireless microphone clipped on the officiant to make sure that everyone can hear the ceremony and the vows. If others are providing readings during the ceremony, another microphone needs to be provided. I traveled by plane and car to a wedding a few years ago in a bucolic setting. The afternoon ceremony was outside with rows of chairs facing the lake. The tent nearby was beautifully set for dinner and dancing. Can I tell you how frustrating it was to not be able to hear the ceremony spoken by the officiant and the bride and groom's vows? With guests coming to support the couple for a special occasion like this, please provide the means for them to hear this important milestone. Even a backyard party may need a microphone and speakers for guests to hear what will be announced.

Musicians or DJs usually have their own sound system, so you could use their microphone for special announcements. Check with them to confirm. Don't hesitate to ask the musicians to turn the volume down if the music is too loud and guests cannot hear each other when talking. Don't be intimidated if you ask the musicians or DJ to turn down the music and they don't turn down the music enough. Go ask again. Insist. It's your party, and you call the shots. You want music to enhance the event, not drive people away because the music is too loud and they can't talk with each other. Remember, the point of any event is to create connections, and every aspect of the event must support that.

HOW TO USE A MICROPHONE

Have you ever watched someone waving their microphone around and you can't hear anything they say? I want to slap my forehead when I see this. The purpose of the amplified microphone is so people can HEAR you. I always recommend to put the microphone on your chin just below your mouth so that when you move your head the microphone goes with you. What a concept! Speak clearly into the microphone and don't speak too fast. Take a deep breath between each sentence. Pause and then continue. You want everyone to hear what you say—and they want to hear YOU!

PRINTED MATERIALS

I am particular about graphics and printed materials for an event, especially when there are a lot of elements to the event or several events over a weekend. Many weddings invite guests for a destination wedding with an arrival gathering the first afternoon or evening. Since everyone is gathering for the first time, help them out and provide name tags for everyone. It makes introductions easier and helps guests remember people's names. I need the help, don't you?

Provide seating assignments with escort cards and place cards at each table to let the guests know you're taking care of them. They are happy to be directed as they are there to support the bride and groom. Be consistent with graphics so all the elements tie together. (Remember, escort cards have the guest's name on the front and on the back or inside (if it's a tent card) it has the name or number of the table where they will be seated. For the wedding reception, it is helpful to also provide escort cards to let guests know where you want them to be seated at the dinner tables. Place cards can be optional if you direct them to their table.

For a wedding ceremony, it is nice to provide a printed program so that everyone knows who is participating.

Graphics to identify an event throughout all printed elements are not limited to weddings. I have done annual business lunches that had the same graphics on the mailed invitations, signage, and table numbers at the lunch consistently every year. Nonprofit galas or smaller events also benefit from graphics that identify the organization and the event. This provides the guests and sponsors with an identifiable visual that is coherent with the branding of the event. Printed materials can include invitations, name tags, place cards, escort cards, flyers, posters, signs, banners, stickers to brand gift bags, file folders or other items, and even T-shirts. There's probably more to add to the list, but you get the idea.

Working with a professional graphic designer over many years, I have benefitted from their expertise and learned a lot along the way. Yes, anyone can create a flyer or other graphics. Will they be as effective? I don't find that they always are.

There are many graphic design principles to keep in mind.

FIRST, provide space on the invitation, sign, flyer, and other materials. If the words are spread all over the page, there is no place for the eye to rest. The copy information is important—and the **space** around the copy, the words—is equally important. It allows the words and information to stand out, AND for the eye to see it. Let's start with the fact that most people don't read. Really!

SECOND, keep your copy short and to the point. You want the words you use to elicit a mood of excitement, expectation, fun, or whatever else you want to get across with the specific information.

And **THIRD, you want to grab the recipient visually**—graphically—about the event when they see the printed material. An effective invitation or other printed materials uses both of these elements—the copy (words) and the graphics. That's where a professional is really worth the investment of time and money. If the event you are planning does not warrant a professional graphic designer, at the very least it is important to understand these principles. Also, remember to use the same font for everything. Consistency is important.

Years ago, I helped a nonprofit create an invitation to their annual gala with a twist. Instead of being super formal, it was "Jeans and Jewels." It was an outdoor event at a winery. This allowed the men to be comfortable in jeans and the women to dress up with jewels however they wished. The visual on the front of the invitation, created by my graphic designer, was instantly appealing and elicited excitement about the event. They had a huge turnout. You want every detail of an invitation to express the focus and purpose of your event. Adding an element of fun and surprise to your invitation helps to catch people's attention, which is what you want. You want them to READ it and say, "I don't want to miss this!" Including an unexpected element of surprise during an event also enhances a memorable experience for your guests.

The overall event design includes all the elements described above. By keeping your vision in mind, you will have created an environment that is consistent with your purpose and goals that reflects the atmosphere and Energy Bubble you have built. This creates a "WOW" experience not only when your guests walk into your event space, but also from the energy and experience they have during your whole event. They will express the qualities you wrote out when you started your planning. It's amazing to see it all manifest!

"Symphony is the ability to put together the pieces . . . and to invent something new by combining elements nobody else thought to pair."

–Daniel Pink, *A Whole New Mind*

Chapter Six

It's Event Day

The day you have been planning for months has finally arrived, and you are now on-site for the setup of this special event. You've planned, prepped, reviewed, made lists, checked off lists, and created a timeline for what needs to be done when—not only on the event day but also on the days leading up to the day. Okay, even if it's a small party in your home, you have still been planning it for a couple of months unless it's impromptu. Let's go with events you have been planning in advance to review here. Remember, before you arrive on-site for event day . . .

It's all about the follow-up, the follow-up!

HOW TO PLAN AND ENJOY YOUR OWN PARTY

I hosted a summer celebration birthday for ten guests to be set up on my large patio. Two months prior to the date, I had emailed friends inviting them for a Saturday in August. A month before the event, I ordered some rentals. I also emailed my guests to reconfirm they were coming. When it's a small gathering with friends, I'm fine asking them to bring something. They are always happy to do so. I asked two friends to bring salads and discussed with them what to make, which would add to what I was providing for the dinner. The other friends I asked to bring an hors d'oeuvre. I found out what hors d'oeuvre each was bringing so there would not be duplicates. Good thing I did as two were going to bring deviled eggs. One platter is fine; two would be a bit much! I provided the entrée, a salad, and the dessert. I refer to this as orchestrating the menu with friends. If you host a potluck, I recommend following up with each person also so you are ensured to have a good variety. I attended a lovely summer lunch one time that was all tomato salads plus the salmon the host provided. Let that be a lesson to orchestrate rather than being surprised!

Friday, the day before the party, I picked up two rental tables and some chairs to make my outdoor table twice as long to accommodate everyone at the table. My outdoor table is sixty inches long, thirty-six inches wide, and 28.5 inches high. The two rental tables were thirty-five inches, square, and twenty-eight inches high.

Everything is an Event

Close enough to make a continuous long dining table for ten.

After I got home, I put the two tables together, and one was not usable. I discovered that the base of one table was wobbly and would not be able to be used. Dang. The rental company, which I had ordered from many times in the past, was now closed and was closed for the weekend. No way for me to get a new table from them. Okay, now what? I live close to Target, so I went online to see what tables they had. I found card tables that were thirty-four-inches square and twenty-eight inches high. This would do. I was at the store the next morning when it opened at 8:00 a.m.—this is my event day!—and purchased two of these card tables. Whew! Table problem solved.

Let me note that I didn't panic because the rental tables would not work. I started to explore what I could do to fix the situation and provide the long table I envisioned for the dinner party. I used my mantra, "It will all get done—in its right way and right time." This is a small example of what happens when there is a snafu in execution. When I returned the tables and chairs to the rental company after the weekend, I got a refund for the tables. I know if I ever order these tables again that I will need to see that they are solid while I am there at the rental company—before I get home—or, if they are delivered, they must put them together before I will let the rental staff leave. Lesson learned.

Back home with my new tables, I set them up next to my outdoor table. *Okay, this works*, I thought. I also put out two tables for the bar and buffet. A friend lent me their six-foot table for the buffet. I "borrowed" my outdoor gardening table to use as the bar. It's very lightweight and easy to move. Now, I needed to cover all the tables so you don't see the legs—or the dirt-stained lower shelf of my gardening table.

Years ago, I ordered cotton muslin from Rose Brand, a theater supply company. They have fabrics that are wider than you can get in a fabric store, and their prices are reasonable. I ordered the lightweight cotton muslin in the seventy-six-inch width (they will ship samples so you can decide what you need). I made six tablecloths about 124 inches long and three cloths about ninety-six inches long. I hemmed the ends on my sewing machine and have used them over and over as tablecloths and to drape over items that need to "disappear." The lengths mentioned are after I hemmed them. Add a couple inches more before cutting the lengths to allow for hemming. They are washable, and I can bleach the natural muslin if needed.

I put a shorter muslin cloth over the gardening table bringing the front of the cloth down to cover the lower shelf. I put a longer muslin cloth over the six-foot buffet table and used two of the longer cloths to cover my "new" long dining table. Over each of the tables, I then added cloths of handwoven ikats I purchased years ago in Bali. They were cotton, so they, too, were washable. Now the focus was on the ikat fabrics on the tops of the tables and not the muslin under-cloths, and the legs of the tables were not visible. It was a very hot day, and I did not have the time to iron the muslin cloths, so there were a few wrinkles. I figured my guests would not be looking at the wrinkles, and no one mentioned anything about them, only exclaiming how wonderful everything looked. With my magic wand, I brought the focus to what I wanted the guests to notice—what was ON the tables, not what was underneath. An example of "Drape It" (see page 94) is to have what you don't want to be seen disappear.

Now to set the tables. The bar included an ice bucket, one basket filled with plastic tumblers, and another basket with plastic champagne flutes. I didn't want any glass breaking on the cement patio. I had a tub for bottles of wine and champagne and another tub with assorted bottles of Hint water. It's always good to have a non-alcoholic option or two available. (Note: I bought these two tubs, one metal, one plastic, years ago and have used them many times. You can find these at stores or online. It's not necessary to pay a lot for them.) One hour before guests arrived, I filled both tubs with ice so the beverages would be chilled and ready. One hour is all you need to chill them. Cocktail napkins were also on the bar. The buffet table was free for the hors d'oeuvres the guests would bring.

1) The bar set up, 2) The under cloth hides the legs and dirty shelf (no one knows!), 3) The buffet with cotton ikat overlay with under cloth to cover the ends of the table.

Everything is an Event

A note about hors d'oeuvres:

Yes, it's a French word. Hors d'oeuvres are finger foods. They should be easy to pick up and not messy to eat. Keep in mind that they need to be one or two bites at the most. These are nibbles to accompany beverages and cocktails. An appetizer is a first course served on a plate. Most restaurants list appetizers on their menus. I find many people use these terms interchangeably, however, they are not the same thing.

I set the dining table with my grandmother's china and silver flatware and used tall jelly glasses for water. Since these glasses were on the table, I wasn't worried about them breaking; however, these are sturdy glasses. I alternated two cotton print blue and white napkins around the table and added small potted mums down the center of the table. I bought small pots of mums a few days earlier and replanted them in terracotta pots—much better looking than the plastic pots they came in.

THE DINNER MENU

Baked Salmon with Sauce Verte
Corn Tomato Basil Salad
Quinoa Salad (brought by a guest)
Mixed Green Salad (brought by a guest)

DESSERT

Chocolate Zucchini Layer Cake
with Chocolate Buttercream Frosting and Raspberry Filling
Fresh Strawberries and Raspberries

A few days before the party, I purchased fresh corn on the cob and beautiful ripe tomatoes at the farmers' market. I also picked up strawberries and raspberries to serve with the cake. The day before the party I cooked the corn, cut it off the cob, and put it in the fridge. Additionally, I made the sauce verte (green sauce—the *New York Times* has a great recipe) for the salmon. For the birthday celebration, I made a chocolate zucchini layer cake. I was given a huge zucchini from a friend's garden, so that was my inspiration for what kind of cake to make. The evening before, I simmered frozen raspberries and then pushed them through a sieve to remove the seeds for a filling for the cake, adding some cornstarch to the puree simmered in a small saucepan to thicken it. Does this sound like I just jumped in and did all these things? Actually, I followed the same plan I have mentioned for any event.

I made an event timeline that outlined when I would go shopping, when to go to the farmers' market, what food to prepare or prep on what day, when to pick up rentals, and what needed to be done on setup event day, so all was planned out in advance. By doing this, I wasn't trying to remember what I needed to do, it was all written down—including the menu.

After setting the tables in the morning, I made the chocolate buttercream frosting, assembled the cake, frosted it, and put it in the fridge. In the early afternoon, I baked a large salmon. I then made the corn tomato basil salad. It's so easy and delicious—chop the tomatoes and the basil and mix with the corn. Add salt and pepper and olive oil and you are done. Tastes like summer! The strawberries and raspberries were rinsed and dried (laid out on towels). I sliced the strawberries in half or quarters, depending on the size, and placed them with the raspberries in a serving bowl. I then put the bowl in the fridge till it was time for dessert. Remember, it was a hot day. Here is a photo of my salmon—from a local fisherman—stuffed with herbs and ready to bake.

Dinner table set. Salmon stuffed and ready to bake.

You might have noticed that I planned a menu where everything was made and ready before the guests arrived. This gives me the ability to be present with my guests instead of doing last-minute fixings. I can also do one more review of all the setup and then relax for a few minutes or more. I like to have time to be dressed and calm before welcoming my guests.

Everyone arrived on time at 5:00 p.m. (I love that), and we gathered on the patio, toasted with champagne, and enjoyed the hors d'oeuvres that they brought. After an hour or so, many hands helped put out the food on the buffet for dinner and filled the water glasses. The green salad was tossed with dressing at the last minute.

Everything is an Event

I served the salmon, and all helped themselves to the sauce verte and the salads. When it was time for dessert, I brought out the cake and the bowl of berries. I was so excited to serve the cake that I forgot to take a picture of the cake before it was cut—oh, well! Let me add that it was delicious!

Guests toast a fun summer evening party gathering. The Chocolate Zucchini Cake with chocolate frosting and raspberry purée filling. Yum!

IT'S EVENT DAY—FOR A **BIGGER** EVENT!

For a large event, there are more details to review. Planning began about nine months prior to the event date. I always say there's a reason gestation is nine months. You need all that time for planning the different parts of the event and the specific details, plus giving space for all to unfold. You have followed up with all pertinent people several times as the date nears. You have emailed and called the caterer, the rental company and staff, or managers, so everyone is on the same page. You have been coordinating with them for months. You reviewed with them your event timeline (sent via email and you now have printed copies on-site to hand out), and you confirmed the guest count for food and rentals a couple weeks ago, reconfirmed arrival times for deliveries, and have phone numbers for everyone on the event timeline. Remember, it's important to have just one place to look for the info when you are on-site. And you may have also reconfirmed with your guests to make sure they know what time to arrive. They might not remember or have read your invitation! This could be phone calls or emails, depending on the circumstances. Remember, **it's all about the follow-up!**

If there are rentals to be delivered or picked up, they are arriving or just arrived the day before. It is important to check the rentals when they arrive to make sure everything is received that you ordered. That means you will be meeting the rental company when they arrive.

112 *Everything is an Event*

What happens on event day? It could start the day before with setup, or much earlier on the event day—way earlier than the usual two hours before start time. A wonderful client I have worked with for many events planned an outdoor party for about seventy guests. As usual, I had selected the caterer, band, valet, rentals, lighting, table floral design (I gave away succulents), and photographer, all with my clients' approval. The rentals were delivered the day before. Yes, I was there to check them in and make sure all was received that was ordered. On the event day, the catering staff arrived four hours prior to the party to set up the dining tables, linen, and chairs and set the tables on the large lawn. There were nine tables of eight. Lights and heaters were also arranged around the tables so when it got dark the yard was lit and guests stayed warm. Buffet tables and a welcome table with escort cards set out alphabetically by the guests' last names provided their table number. There was also a "screen" made with fabric draped to remove the caterer's work area from view that was created by the staff. No need for guests to see behind the scenes. This is a great example of "drape it."

1) Drape It to hide the catering staff working behind the scenes, 2) The buffet set and ready for guests, 3) Escort cards set out for the guests,

As the event manager, I was on-site when the staff arrived to oversee that the setup was done correctly and make sure that the timing of the event moved forward as planned. I was constantly coordinating with the catering manager and chef. As guests began to arrive, I helped welcome them and invited them to pick up their escort cards to then find their table. It's good to remember that many guests like to put their wraps and handbags at their table, freeing them to enjoy cocktails and passed hors d'oeuvres. Watching the timing, I checked in with the catering manager to see when the food would be ready for the buffet. Now, it was time for me to go around to the guests and let them know the buffet was open. Wait staff were positioned at the buffet to serve the guests. Having servers allowed for the

Everything is an Event 113

buffet line to move quickly and easily so no one was waiting a long time in line. Monitoring the tables, I assessed when it was the right time to have the staff clear the dinner plates from the guests' tables. What's next on the schedule? Dessert? Dancing with music from the band? Or both? It depends on the plan. The dessert buffet could be open with coffee and tea service for those ready before they start dancing. Others might take a break from dancing and then get their dessert and coffee. A buffet service allows for flexibility and choices.

1) The clients' yard set up with dinner tables, lighting and heaters around the dance floor, 2) A table setting with centerpiece of succulent plants and candle, 3) A view of the garden that surrounds the lawn and party area.

Oh, and then as I say, *it's not over when it's over*. When the guests departed, the catering staff cleared the tables, collected the linens, broke down the tables and chairs, and stacked them so that all was ready for the rental company to come and collect the rentals the next day. I was not there when they picked up the rentals, however, I did follow up with them—and the client—via phone to make sure everything was picked up. The clients told me, once again as they have with other parties, "Thank you for letting us be guests at our own great party, completely carefree, knowing that you had taken care of everything."

A LARGE NONPROFIT GALA

Maybe you volunteer for a nonprofit organization. Do you help with their annual event? Volunteer committees many times help with the details that make a big difference at an event. Or perhaps you attend an organization's gala to support their work in your community. Have you ever wondered how the event comes together before you arrive at the party? Of course, there are nine to ten months of advanced planning before on-site setup begins. It takes many vendors contracted to execute the plans. They all play their part in bringing the gala to fruition. The following is a description of how a large gala unfolds on-site.

I have provided pro bono event consulting for a nonprofit organization, Lifehouse Agency, for many years on their annual award-winning gala fundraiser, Great Chefs & Wineries. Lifehouse provides support to adults and teens with intellectual and developmental disabilities living in the Bay Area, and has been doing so for over seventy years. My sister's last few years of life were made so much better by their 24/7 caring staff in a wonderful home environment. In gratitude, I have consulted with them on their event, Great Chefs & Wineries, and also managed the event on-site. This event was already a widely attended special event when I started working with them. I addressed how it could be improved to make something great even better. First, more organization. Remember, order creates greater calm and peace of mind. I created an event timeline, which they had not had, which provided the CEO and everyone else with certainty of what would happen when. Second was raising the bar of the visibility of WHY guests were attending this great event—not just for the fabulous food and wines, but to support the clients that Lifehouse cared for.

Remember, this was actually a **FUNraiser** and **FRIENDraiser**. Building relationships is key for any event, and this one was focused on inviting and appreciating their major sponsors, table sponsors, and guests—many of whom had supported this event for many years, plus also adding new sponsors and guests as they learned about Lifehouse.

Okay, now to the setup. With this large of an event for 500 guests, setup began two days before the event with the large tent being installed where the two-hour feast of twenty-five restaurants serving hors d'oeuvres and twenty-five wineries pouring wine would occur. The day before the event, more setup continued with event staff setting up tables in the tent, placing fifty tables of ten in the dining room, dressing them with linen, and setting the tables with flatware, glassware, plates, and napkins. This day also began with the technical team setting up the stage, lighting, and sound.

The volunteer planning committee arrived in the afternoon to place all the materials at each table. There were auction catalogs and auction paddles for the live auction on each table. Table stands with sponsor names were put on the corresponding tables. Small cards with clients' photos and a short statement about Lifehouse were placed in front of each guest's table setting. This connected the dots with WHY

Everything is an Event

guests were at this event. There were lots of details to check to make sure all was correct. Most of the setup was completed by around 6:00 p.m. Ready for the gala the next day.

On the gala event day, volunteers and staff arrived about four to five hours prior to the event start time. Beautiful floral centerpieces were added to the fifty round tables. Plus, more preparation in the tent for the Wine & Dine Reception prior to the restaurants arriving to serve their hors d'oeuvres and wineries arriving to pour their wine. Signs were hung above each table with their company name. You would think that this was plenty of time for everything to get done. It was, but time goes faster than you think when there are so many details to be addressed. Staff in management positions needed to sign out their walkie-talkies, volunteers needed instructions for what their roles were, and catering staff were also prepping food for the cheese course and dessert.

Table setting for the Great Chefs & Wineries Gala

Once the event began, guests started arriving, checking in, being welcomed, and invited to join the reception to enjoy the restaurants' hors d'oeuvres and wines being poured. Did I mention I had the event timeline on my clipboard, referring to each item as we moved through the timing of the event? I was also on a walkie-talkie with event staff to make sure catering staff were picking up plates and glasses so they wouldn't pile up during the Wine & Dine reception. I let them know which winery needed more ice or which restaurant needed more plates. I roamed through the space, constantly checking on everything. After the two-hour reception, which was really dinner with all those delicious hors d'oeuvres and much wine tasting, there was an announcement inviting guests into what we called the ballroom. A cheese course platter was at each guest's table. The Wine & Dine area cleared as restaurants and wineries departed and things quieted down a bit for me, but not for the CEO who was now on the stage welcoming guests and inviting other speakers to the stage. More actions unfolded, all listed on the event timeline and planned and reviewed many times before we were on-site. A main highlight was next with a group of about eight clients performing a dance to an upbeat song, which they had been practicing for months. This always brings guests to their feet, applauding the lively performance. Dessert was served, and the live auction came next with amazing items highlighted on large screens. After the auction, a fabulous band arrived on the stage and set everyone to dancing. A great way to end an evening with amazing support for the organization.

And . . . then there was breakdown. There was a dedicated crew that managed the setup and manages the breakdown. What goes up must come down! The tables and linen in the tent were broken down while guests were in the ballroom. Now, it was time to collect all the glassware, flatware, napkins, and linen and break down the dining tables and chairs. These rentals were counted to make sure the correct rental items were being returned. The rental company arrived the next morning to load up the tables, chairs, linen, etc. and break down the tent. Lifehouse staff drove a truck loaded with items that went back to their office. Whew! Lots of moving pieces. Time for a massage!

WHAT HAPPENS FOR A WEDDING?

Weddings are very special events. They are planned over months and even years before this day when reserving a date and a location. There are so many details that make up a ceremony and celebration, all with the intention of bringing everyone together in support of the couple and surrounding them with love. A wedding usually includes several events, including the rehearsal dinner, the ceremony, and the reception.

Whether the wedding includes thirty-five people or 350, the planning and principles remain the same. Starting with what? The intention for the **experience** that the bride and groom want for themselves and for their guests. The clarity about what qualities they want to be present for the day or days of celebration is the starting point for all planning. Remember, this is the foundation upon which all plans, ideas, and details are built. The first question I always ask wedding clients is, **"What is the experience you want to have?"**

Do you need a wedding planner for your wedding? Good question. As this is a once-in-a-lifetime event, it's best to have guidance. This doesn't mean you need a wedding professional to handle it all unless you do want that. However, I recommend consulting with a wedding planner when you decide to get married. Maybe you have found the location and the date—always important to get these nailed down. Many

Everything is an Event

times, it's a year in advance to get the location and date you want. Now, before you start planning all the specifics, sit down for a consultation. I have consulted with clients on weddings they were planning themselves, and they discovered that our meeting made all the difference in how their wedding turned out. I have met with a bride and groom several times to review plans and to create their event timeline, or sometimes just once to review where they are in the planning or before they start planning. I ask questions they hadn't thought of. I have recommended resources, caterers, and florists for them to check out and remind them of what is necessary in their plans. Having an overall picture of what is required helps create a clearer plan. As mentioned before, the principle is *order creates greater calm and peace of mind.*

Many brides who have planned their own weddings decide they need a day-of wedding coordinator. Most brides DO realize that they cannot manage their wedding events as they have ONE JOB that day—being the bride! However, I never agree to be on-site just for the day of the wedding. Why? Without knowing all the plans, communications, and agreements with vendors, the intention for the day, and how the flow of timing is desired and planned, I cannot promise to oversee what they want to unfold. Showing up just before the event starts is not a recipe for success. Everything needs to be reviewed during several meetings so I am aware of everything that the bride and groom want for their day.

Most weddings have a rehearsal and rehearsal dinner the day before the wedding and reception. **One thing to always remember, for every event, and especially for weddings, is to take care of the guests.** After the wedding ceremony, it is important to create the time and space for guests to congratulate the bride and groom at the beginning of the reception. A formal reception line is not necessary; however, allowing guests to come up and speak to the couple is necessary as they will do this whether you plan for it or not. So, plan for it. Allow time in the schedule for the guests to embrace the bride and groom. I always recommend that the couple place themselves in the room so they are in a space where it is easy for their guests to line up (yes, they will do this!). Also, have a table behind the bride and groom with easy access to glasses of champagne or other beverages.

If there is a ceremony, whether in a church or a special location, it is best to review the program, the timing, what music is desired, and what musicians are needed. Many times, I have helped design the program for the ceremony with the intention of having a smooth flow of one element moving to the next. I have recommended musicians that might work for the ceremony or found musicians that the bride and groom wanted. I am behind the scenes to coach the bridal party for when each person is to walk down the aisle. This is usually practiced the night before at the ceremony rehearsal. I have also coordinated with the florist for their timing of decorating the church or special location and reception and delivering the bouquets and boutonnieres for the wedding party. I will also make sure that each boutonniere is pinned and bouquets are given to each member of the bridal party.

A FORMAL SAN FRANCISCO WEDDING

I planned and coordinated a large wedding for 240 guests many years ago with a ceremony that was held in a beautiful Catholic church in San Francisco and a reception at a famous Nob Hill hotel. The rehearsal at the church was at 5:30 p.m. two days before the wedding instead of the usual night before. After the practice of everyone walking down the aisle a couple times, everyone adjourned for a lovely dinner at a restaurant in Sausalito. I arranged the place cards and menu cards on the dinner tables and set the escort cards on a table by the entrance.

Saturday, the morning of the wedding day, I picked up the bouquet for the bride to use for photographs and stephanotis for her hair. I arrived at the hotel, delivered the flowers to the bride, and then gave my hotel contact the place cards, menu cards, escort cards, and the floor plan. Need I mention that the seating arrangements had been planned, reviewed, and finalized many days in advance?! The photographer arrived just before noon to take pictures of the bride and bridesmaids getting ready.

The groom and groomsmen arrived at the hotel at 12:30 p.m. A room was set aside for them to get dressed. Sandwiches and beverages were provided. You have to keep everyone fed! A bus for the bridal party and limousines for the parents of the bride and groom had been arranged to bring them from the hotel to the church. I arrived at the church at the same time as the bridal party at 2:00 p.m. and distributed bouquets, boutonnieres, and corsages. I taped paper over the glass doors so guests arriving in the lobby could not see into the church while the photographer took pictures of the bridal party.

The florist had placed ribbons and bows with flowers at the ends of the pews along the center aisle and beautiful large floral arrangements at the altar. While we arrived at the church, the florist was now at the hotel placing floral centerpieces on each dinner table with beautiful calligraphed table name banners displayed above each centerpiece.

A Word About Wedding Photographs

There are two main options for wedding day photographs.

1) Take pictures of the bride and groom and wedding party AFTER the ceremony, which means that the groom doesn't see the bride until she walks down the aisle.

2) Have photographs taken BEFORE the wedding ceremony of the bride, groom, and wedding party. Some object to this because they want the surprise of the "reveal" on the aisle. Others opt to have a private meeting of the bride and groom—an intimate reveal for the couple—before photos and then the ceremony.

With all the weddings I have coordinated over many years, I found that the time spent with the photographer after the wedding and before the reception creates a time when all the guests are basically waiting for the bridal couple to show up after the ceremony. Yes, they are all at the reception, however, the main players are missing. All the guests are there to support the couple, and they are not around. Sometimes, it's quite a wait with photos being taken at several locations. I really think option number two is a better way to take care of the bridal couple and the guests. After the reception is also a good time to take group photos of family with the bridal couple. Everyone is relaxed and is just fine with watching the photos being taken.

After all the photographs of the wedding party were completed around the church altar, it was time for the groomsmen to take their places to usher guests to their seats. Music began playing, and I removed the paper covering the glass doors and opened them for guests to begin entering the church.

While the ceremony was transpiring, the musicians arrived to set up in the reception room. When the bridal couple and their parents arrived at the hotel, they had about ten minutes in a separate room for photos. There were also drinks and hors

The Bride and her parents, the Bridal table, a calligraphed place card

d'oeuvres set out for them. You've got to keep everyone fed! With music playing, the reception began. The bridal couple and both sets of parents formed the receiving line and they welcomed guests as they arrived. The bar was open and hors d'oeuvres were passed by hotel wait staff. I was positioned at the entry table with the escort cards to let the guests know where their tables were in the dining room.

After an hour and a quarter, the ballroom doors opened, and guests were invited to find their tables. The room was set with dinner tables on either end of a large dance floor with a stage for the band and a long wedding party table opposite the stage and dance floor. Calligraphed place cards were set out at each place, and two menu cards were at each table. This was a very elegant affair with so much thought about every detail. Who was seated at each table was considered so that each guest connected with people they knew or didn't know they needed to know. The bride's parents seated me at a table with people I knew and several I didn't. However, three years later, I ended up marrying a lovely English gentleman who was at my table. I didn't remember meeting him then as I was up and down all night managing the event. A year later, the bride's parent reintroduced us. That's another story told in my book *The Grief Train: A healing journey of love, loss and renewal*.

After guests were seated at their tables, the bride and groom made their entrance into the ballroom for a first dance, which also started a dance set, which got everyone up to dance. This was an evening of fabulous food and amazing music with a Motown band. No one could stay seated when they started singing and playing! Dance sets were planned between service of courses. It unfolded like this:

A table setting and an elegant wedding cake.

Everything is an Event

6:00 p.m.	Bride & groom arrive to dance floor, first dance & dance set
	Wait staff served bread and wine to the tables
6:30 p.m.	Father of the bride welcomed everyone from the stage; please be seated for dinner.
	First course served
	Entrée served
7:25 p.m.	Toasts by the best man and maid-of-honor from the stage
7:35 p.m.	Dance set starting with father/daughter, mother/son dance, & everyone then joining on the dance floor
	Wait staff clears tables, serves salad course
8:00 p.m.	Salad & wine is enjoyed by guests
8:15 p.m.	Dance set
8:45 p.m.	Guests take their seats. Bride & groom on stage, give toasts, then cut the cake
9:10 p.m.	Dance set
	Cake is plated and served
9:55 p.m.	Bride tosses bouquet from the stage
10:30 p.m.	Bride & groom depart, reception concludes

Does it sound like too much dancing? Well, maybe, but I can say the dance floor was filled! Nobody could stay in their seats! When the bridal couple departs, that's always the signal for the conclusion of the event. As the guests departed, they were handed a gift box of dragée (drah-zhay), sugar-coated almonds, a classic wedding favor.

The end result of this wedding? People had so much fun celebrating—dancing to the music by the band AND enjoying the fabulous food! It was definitely an evening of a warm, loving, joyful embrace of the couple. The toasts were heartfelt and short.

> **A Word About Toasts:**
>
> It's not fair to all your guests to have anyone and everyone come up to the microphone and say something to toast the bride and groom. That's even more important if it's a large wedding. This should be orchestrated so that those who speak are prepared. Usually, it's the best man and maid of honor who give the toasts. Maybe also the father of the bride. Keep it to three, max four, people for the toasts. With the wedding outlined above, there were toasts sprinkled throughout the evening, and it was planned who was to speak and when. Planning is the key with toasts!

When the bridal couple departed the reception for their room at the hotel, I made sure that dinner, snacks, and beverages were in their room. The bride and groom don't always get a chance to eat much during their reception. Yes, you have to keep everyone fed! There were wedding gifts brought by guests to the reception, which had to be taken care of. I followed up to make sure they were put in the bridal suite, which had been agreed to beforehand.

The wedding described above was a big one with lots of details and planning. You may not be planning such a formal affair; however, I hope this provides ideas to incorporate for your own wedding. There are no rules to follow today, so you can design your wedding as you desire. It can be as informal or formal as you would like.

I love the stories of parties that guests were invited to where the surprise was that the bride and groom got married. It appeared impromptu, but we know it wasn't! I once coordinated a wedding where everyone, starting with the bride and groom, was dressed in medieval costumes. Another wedding was a simple ceremony in the client's lovely garden followed by a lunch in her living room for the twenty-five guests.

AN AT-HOME WEDDING—ELAINE AND LYMAN

At-home weddings can be formal or very informal. It's a choice. It depends on how many guests you have and especially what experience the bride and groom want for themselves and their guests. Elaine and Lyman planned a formal affair and were involved with every aspect of their wedding ceremony and reception held at their lovely home in the hills of Marin County.

A weekend of events was planned as there were many guests coming from out of town. I reserved a block of rooms at a nearby hotel. Friday's rehearsal and dinner were planned for thirty family members and close friends. Saturday's late afternoon wedding ceremony and Reception was designed for 100 guests, and a casual Sunday brunch for a smaller group of family and out-of-town friends allowed all to gather one more time. Elaine and Lyman planned to remove the furniture in the large family room for the Friday dinner and Sunday brunch.

I started working on the plans six months in advance of the June wedding. This was plenty of time as the location was their home. If you reserve a wedding space, usually, this is booked a year in advance. I got busy lining up the vendors needed. A graphic designer to design the wedding invitation and other things such as table name cards, escort cards, place cards, and a program for the ceremony, all tied into the same look as the designed invitation. A caterer was needed for all three days' events, and they also arranged for all the rentals required. A lighting company was important to create lighting in the outdoor garden that was beautiful and effective. A florist was hired to provide arrangements in the house and outside in the garden—plus a wedding bouquet and boutonnieres. Classical musicians were requested for the ceremony and a great band for dancing. Valet parking was needed as the house is on a steep hill for the ease of the guests. Of course, a photographer was essential to capture the day, and a calligrapher needed to be found to address the wedding invitations.

Much thought went into all the details and planning as you can gather. Elaine and Lyman reviewed all the plans so all was in alignment with how they envisioned the weekend to look and feel. Every minute of the three days was planned and reviewed using my event timeline. Yes, we did Time Travel to do the event before the event! All the spaces in the home to be used both—inside and out—were thought through for ease of flow to accommodate all the guests. I created floor plans for each of the spaces so that it was clear how everything would be set up, which I shared with the caterer and other vendors. I also shared the event timeline with all pertinent vendors.

Building a Budget:

When I start working with a client, one of the first things I am asked is, "How much is this going to cost?" That's not a question that can be answered right off the bat. First, I need to know what they want their wedding to look and feel like and what they envision for the day or the weekend. I have to build a budget based on what they want. And then we need to review the costs for each aspect of the event and, perhaps, make some hard choices of what they really want and what their budget will allow. Remember, the more people you invite, the more expenses there will be. The cost for 100 guests for food and rentals is not going to be as much as the cost for 250 guests, plus you need a much bigger space for that larger crowd. Costs do vary, and there are always creative ways to keep the cost down. Planning just a wedding day ceremony and reception instead of a three-day weekend affair is one option. There are many options to consider.

Weather is a factor with outdoor weddings. Is a tent needed? I had reserved a tent with the rental company, and on Thursday before the Saturday wedding, I conferred with Elaine and Lyman and it was decided that the weather would be beautiful, so no tent was needed. I called the rental company and canceled it. Thursday began the action with the rentals—tables, chairs, dishes, glassware, flatware, linens, napkins, etc.— delivered in the afternoon. The florist arrived to arrange flowers in many rooms in the house as well as in the garden.

Friday morning, the lighting crew arrived to set up lights in the outdoor garden. It's always good for everyone to be able to see when the sun goes down for safety. The florist arrived to set up the floral border in the garden and for the ceremony backdrop. They also brought flowering potted plants for the rehearsal dinner table centerpieces for that evening. The caterer arrived at 3:30 p.m. to prepare for the rehearsal dinner. For out-of-town guests, a shuttle bus was reserved to bring them from the hotel to the bride and groom's home arriving around 5:30–6:00 p.m. along with family members also arriving at that time. I had set out name tags, which definitely helped everyone get to know each other more easily. The rehearsal was in the garden with a beautiful vista of tree-covered hills in the background. After the rehearsal, everyone gathered in the living room for hors d'oeuvres and beverages. It was a small group of thirty in attendance, so after half an hour, I invited the guests to be seated for dinner in the family room. There were place cards set out at each of the three round tables. A delicious dinner was served family style, which means platters of each entrée and side are placed on the tables for the guests to help themselves. After a lovely gathering including dessert and coffee, the guests departed around 9:30 p.m. The shuttle bus was there to take guests back to the hotel.

Saturday afternoon, I arrived at 1:30 p.m., the same time as the caterer. They unloaded all their food, equipment, etc. and started prepping. At 2:00 p.m., the stylist arrived to fix the bride's hair and make-up. At 3:30 p.m., the band and the photographer arrived. The classical trio showed up shortly after the photographer. The valet team arrived at 4:00 p.m., ready to park the guests' cars. A second photographer arrived and started setting up her table for the "guest book" activity. Instead of a book for guests to sign, each guest or couple was photographed. The photographer printed out the photos and taped them to 8.5"x11" parchment card stock. Guests were then invited to come back to the table and write a message to the bride and groom. At the end of the evening, I collected all the photos with well wishes and put them in a special book for the bride and groom. The guests arrived at 4:30 p.m., including those via the shuttle bus, so all would be ready for the wedding ceremony at 5:00 p.m. The photographer took photos throughout the afternoon and evening capturing the atmosphere, the ceremony, the celebration, and all. The request by Elaine and Lyman was for there to be many informal photographs rather than formal group shots.

It was a beautiful clear day. The classical trio began playing in the garden at 4:30 p.m., and guests started gathering for the ceremony. The chairs were arranged in curved rows, which helped everyone feel more connected and allowed them to see each other—much better than straight rows of chairs. As the guests stepped out into the garden, I handed out paper umbrellas for those who wanted shade from the sun. (We anticipated that the sun would be shining, so I had ordered the paper umbrellas online.) A basket of rings was set out with a card that read, "*Please take one of these rings for your participation in the ceremony.*" When it was time for the

1) The wedding arch and a view of the surrounding mountains, 2) The ceremony chairs set up in curved rows, 3) Umbrellas ready for the sun during the ceremony.

ring exchange during the ceremony, all the guests were asked to hold up their rings—a symbol of love and commitment—bringing everyone together to support the couple. (This ring ceremony including all the guests was requested by Lyman. I bought the 100 steel rings at the hardware store and had the graphic designer create the card.)

After the ceremony, the bride and groom led everyone up the stairs and out the front door to the front patio where a bar was set up, and drinks and hors d'oeuvres were passed. The classical trio moved to the front patio to play during the cocktail reception, which was planned for an hour and a half so that all could have time to congratulate Elaine and Lyman.

While the cocktail reception was going on, the ceremony space was turned into the dinner and dancing space. It's called turning the room, remember? Although this time the "room" was outdoors. Round tables were set with floral centerpieces and votive candles. Space heaters were placed around the tables to keep the guests comfortable when the temperature cooled down at sunset. Elaine, the thoughtful bride, wanted wraps for the guests in case they got cold, so I had purchased fluffy shawls and filled two baskets, which were set outside for guests to help themselves.

The band started playing at 7:00 p.m., and Elaine and Lyman led everyone from the cocktail reception down the stairs and out to the garden for dinner. I guess you've noticed that when the bride and groom take the lead, the guests follow. At a table before going outside to the garden, the guests picked up their escort cards so they would know which table to sit at. Each table had a name card displayed above the centerpiece. Do help guests out by planning the seating so they don't have to figure out where to sit. They want to be told where to go and what to do. Really!

1) The sign above the basket of rings presented for each guest to take one before the ceremony, 2) The ceremony space turned into the dinner and dancing space, 3) Escort cards set out for the guests to pick up as they entered the garden for dinner.

Everything is an Event

After enjoying the dinner, the bride and groom stepped onto the dance floor for their first dance. They then invited all to join them. After some great dancing to the band, there were toasts, and the cake was cut. The catering staff served the cake with chocolate-dipped strawberries on each plate and poured coffee and tea. More dancing ensued, and guests departed around 11:00 p.m.

But wait, there's more! With weddings that include out-of-town guests, it's nice to serve brunch the next day. The caterer and staff arrived at 9:00 a.m. to prep the food and set the tables with new linen in the family room. The lighting crew arrived to take down all the lighting outside in the garden and were gone in an hour. Breakdown always takes less time than setup. Family and close friends arrived at 11:00 a.m. for the brunch buffet, which was a wonderful way to extend the wedding weekend. All departed around 1:00 p.m. The catering staff then collected and stacked the rentals from all three days' events, so everything was ready to be picked up the next day by the rental company.

At the brunch, there were many who said this was the best wedding they had ever attended. Those rave reviews of the "best wedding ever" continued to be received by Elaine and Lyman for months after their wedding. With all the care that Elaine and Lyman had put into their planning and intentions for their weekend, plus the atmosphere being designed to be one of love, connection, family, celebration, fun, and joy . . . the memories and buzz did indeed follow!

The most important thing to remember is . . .

PRINCIPLE #15:
TAKE CARE OF EVERYONE

Keep this important principle in mind during all the thinking and planning you do for any event. Be kind and as the host always think about what your guests may need. Anticipate! The qualities you want your guests to experience in your Energy Bubble exercise includes taking care of everyone.

For a wedding, this includes the bridal couple, guests, band, vendors—all who are part of the event. If there are children in the wedding or included in your event, make sure you take care of making them comfortable by providing a special activity or other age-appropriate ways to keep them entertained. **Take care of everyone—everything else is a detail.**

Many wedding couples plan an after-party. After the wedding ceremony and reception, a small group of friends are invited in advance to meet at another location to continue the celebration. Again, this requires planning ahead to book the location, sending invitations to friends to join the fun, and confirming the number of guests for the evening gathering.

The morning after brunch is another part of the event for many couples. It is an important way for everyone to come together one more time before everyone departs. Depending on the location, this could be as simple as bagels with all the trimmings, or a seated brunch at a restaurant or hotel, or it could be catered at a family's home. Lots of options. When guests come from out of town, it's nice to give them one more way to connect before they head home.

Okay, what about the last-minute wedding or the last-minute planning?

I got a call from a friend saying she needed my help. Her daughter's wedding was canceled at Yosemite because it was closed with all the snow, and the wedding was now at her house the next week! She was in a tizzy. She needed a wedding photographer. I quickly reached out to a wonderful photographer, Stephanie, and connected her with my friend. I was thrilled to find out they hired Stephanie. One challenge handled. The wedding was going to be a small, intimate affair with about fifteen guests. What else did she need to do? A cake was confirmed, and they planned a simple brunch menu of sandwiches and salads after the 11:00 a.m. wedding ceremony by the huge redwood tree in her back yard.

We spent an hour on Zoom. I reviewed the setup outside with chairs to be arranged in a semi-circle for the ceremony. A semi-circle allows the guests to see everyone—much better than in a straight line. In the conversation, she discovered she had enough chairs and didn't have to rent any (shop at home!). We reviewed the setup in the house with a place for the cake and brunch food on the dining table. Seating in the living room would work to accommodate all. Then, we walked through the timing for the day so that everything unfolded in an orderly and easy manner. At the end of the hour, my friend felt so much better. She was calm and getting excited about her daughter's wedding day. Remember, order creates greater calm and peace of mind! How did it all turn out? It was a wonderful, joyful, beautiful celebration of the couple with much heartfelt sharing among all who were there to support the bride and groom. What more could anyone ask for?!

Everything is an Event

> "Design is not just what it looks like and feels like. Design is how it works."
>
> –Steve Jobs

Chapter Seven
Virtual Events

Moving to virtual events was not a gradual shift but a sudden requirement if an event was to be held at all when the COVID-19 pandemic hit the U.S. in March 2020. After seven months of planning an annual two-day conference, we were all in lockdown. The hotel closed, so no event at the hotel. We—the volunteer committee and I—started having meetings on Zoom. It was decided that we would take a week to ask the confirmed forty speakers if they would go virtual with us. We also asked our sponsors if they would go virtual. Our conference is known for the connections people can make with fellow peers, speakers, and sponsors. How could we make that happen virtually? During this week, while committee members reached out to speakers and sponsors, I was trying to envision what a virtual conference would look like and feel like. I had to throw out the picture of what was going to be and invent something new.

> **I fell back on the principles I have always used and explained in this book. First, clarity of purpose. The purpose remains the same even if it's virtual.**

I wrote a three-page paper describing what the event would be like and what the flow would be for this new virtual event so I could visualize it. This reminded me of when I prepare a proposal for a client; I describe what their event will look and feel like so they get a sense of my understanding of their vision. I shared the three-page document with the committee to help them visualize this different event, too. In writing this, I realized that we needed an entirely different team. Everything was technical because it wasn't physical.

The committee met a week later—via Zoom—to discuss the options: go ahead with a virtual conference or cancel it. The report was that almost all the speakers said yes, they would go virtual. More than two-thirds of the sponsors said yes. So, with all the work already done in preparation—confirming speakers and their topics, and the support of our sponsors—it was decided to go ahead and produce the two-day conference virtually. It was going to be too costly to cancel after all that had been done and all the money that had been spent on planning. We would be in a financial hole if we canceled.

With the go-ahead from the committee, I gathered our team—key players from the committee, and our webmaster. My core team and I now pivoted to a virtual conference. We had six weeks!

Although the "venue" changed to virtual, *the purpose of the conference did not change—* **to provide excellence in advanced education and to foster community.**

Creating ways to connect virtually was more challenging, and I had to explore ways to add networking to the program. With this short planning window, we used most of the original schedule for the two days and inserted in scheduled times for attendees to network with the sponsors.

We hired a tech team that could handle the Zoom meetings for all the speakers. We hired another company that could take care of the CE credits for the attendees. We—actually, the technology-oriented part of our team—figured out how to cobble together the technology pieces required to make the conference work virtually. I kept asking questions and looking at the big picture of what we needed to do to make this happen. We had six weeks to invent, create, design, and implement a new event. I'd never put together a new event in six weeks, but that was the goal and the intention as the event dates were not changing.

The role of the event designer is to hold the vision throughout all the planning and execution of an event.

I started a project timeline for the six weeks we had to create the event. I ended up not even looking at it. I didn't have time to write a timeline; I only had time for actions. Every day, we were reviewing what would work, how it could work, and then figuring out what we needed to do to make it happen. Each day revealed something we hadn't known before that needed to be addressed and solved. I realized that my event timeline was worthless for this online event. I had to make a production schedule. Every minute—every second—needed to be planned. It was like producing a TV show. Actually, it wasn't like producing a TV show; it WAS a TV show—called a virtual conference! There were commercials, which were short, thirty-second videos that we asked our sponsors to provide so we could promote and highlight them. We posted these videos on our website sponsor page. We added short fifteen-minute sponsor networking sessions where sponsors shared educational information. The feedback from the attendees afterward was that they learned more about the sponsors and their services in these short presentations than they would have if they chatted with them at their table in person.

We were building the train as it was moving down the track to the event dates. Lots of long hours—sixteen to eighteen hours a day—and continual reinvention was required. Because we had no idea how the internet would work for people, we had most of the speakers pre-record their presentations and committee members pre-recorded their introductions. I wrote and reviewed scripts for the committee chair for each day. I reviewed pre-recorded videos. I had our graphics person create slides that introduced the speakers, slides that listed the codes required for the CE credit, and slides for our sponsors. I was a producer, making sure all the pieces and parts came together for the "show." I've always been a producer of events; this was just a different "venue"—online, virtual, and timed to the minute.

I've never felt such relief to have an event conclude than I did for this one. We did it. We made it happen! I can report that the conference turned out to be very successful. Many were skeptical about it being virtual and were pleasantly surprised at the result. I received numerous responses from attendees and sponsors thanking me and our committee for making it happen. They appreciated the effort required to pull it off so well. It actually then became a model for others in the industry to follow. Things that we had done turned up in other conferences. We were the first to show what a virtual conference could be. Who knew? We were too busy making it happen!

Because this was all virtual, we decided to add two weeks of on-demand sessions for attendees with the opportunity to earn more CE credits by watching recorded sessions and taking a test. These sessions were very popular and were greatly appreciated by the attendees. We decided we needed to keep this addition going forward for the next year.

VIRTUAL MEETINGS

Just like every event, there is always a purpose for a meeting, and everyone attending needs to be clear about the purpose. Zoom meetings have become ubiquitous since the pandemic. I like them better than phone calls because you can see who you are talking to. Yes, the boxes can be small sometimes, but there is a connection that is easier than on the phone. Plus, you know everyone is focused on the meeting. With conference calls, how do you know? I appreciate the technology that lets us connect with each other on Zoom (or other platforms such as Google, Webex, and others). It certainly saved the day for us all during the time of staying at home.

There's another important aspect to meetings and events. They need to start on time! For events, it's showtime that has been planned and needs to start at the time as promised. For meetings, they also need to start on time AND end on time. Why? It's respectful of everyone's time. It is important to be considerate of others and their time. It's also professional and reflects the intention to focus on the purpose of the meeting. Providing an agenda before the meeting is important. It gives everyone a clear idea of what needs to be discussed and allows everyone to be prepared. In the agenda, I list the topics to be discussed, who will be introducing the conversation about each topic, and an estimated time for each topic. It could be ten minutes or fifteen minutes—or more, or less. Sometimes it's five minutes or thirty minutes depending on the topic. Being specific on the agenda lets everyone know what to expect and they can see the meeting is scheduled to end on time.

Prior to the meeting, I check in with those who will address updates in their area of responsibility so they are prepared to speak at the meeting. Also, it is key to have someone lead the meeting to keep the discussions on track. The person leading the meeting—the committee chair, team lead, or the event professional—manages the time and moves the meeting along. If a conversation gets bogged down, the leader can suggest they take it offline and report back via email or at the next meeting.

I'm a stickler for meetings starting on time and ending when they are scheduled to end. No dragging things on and on. If the meeting concludes earlier than originally scheduled after all items have been reviewed and discussed, it's a win-win for everyone.

PROJECT TIMELINES FOR VIRTUAL EVENTS

As mentioned previously, in planning an event I create a project timeline that notes all the actions needed to be taken over the months of planning to arrive at the event dates. The project timeline is created at the start of a project and continually updated. For my annual conference event, the meeting dates are scheduled for the whole ten months prior to the event and reviewed with the committee, where necessary, to make sure everyone can be present. Bringing the committee or team's presence to the meetings contributes energy and attention to the intention of the event. Regular monthly meetings with the committee or team are imperative so that 1) everyone can share what they have accomplished during the past few weeks, 2) to ensure that all are kept up to date with progress and any glitches that have arisen, and 3) to keep all moving forward as planned. Regularly meeting together is essential because new ideas or additional aspects of the event are revealed in the conversations.

It is helpful to start meetings with each person checking in or answering a question the chair has posed. It's really about putting everyone's "voice in the room" and bringing everyone's energy together in the present. This is something to do whether the meeting is virtual or in person. As I began to plan future client meetings during the pandemic, I was scheduling our committee meetings to be virtual via Zoom. This meant that everyone stayed safe plus no one needed to spend time traveling. There is ease to be able to just schedule the meeting time and not having to travel. I always claim ease for all my events, remember?!

MOVING FORWARD—ANOTHER VIRTUAL YEAR

As we began to plan in the fall of 2020 for the 2021 conference, with the pandemic still keeping people home, we determined that a virtual conference was the only option. This time, we had the usual ten months to plan and make it better. A lot was learned from the first virtual conference, and there were many more options and ideas now available. Instead of two long days, we scheduled three shorter days. The program was designed to provide more breaks, more opportunities to network with others, and shorter days for less screen fatigue. And technology improved tremendously in just six months, so we could streamline the technology to one main virtual venue platform, which thus provided a much easier experience for the speakers, sponsors, and attendees. Having had most sessions pre-recorded last year, we decided we could go live with all the sessions for this year. And yes, we added the on-demand sessions again for two weeks after the three-day live virtual conference, allowing attendees to get more CE credits.

As mentioned throughout this book, any event is really about the experience. That doesn't change just because we are now in front of a screen. The language may change but the intent is still the same. We want to connect with others and engagement is the term being used. How to keep those watching the screen engaged? There are polls that can be added during speaker presentations, Q&A at the end of the presentations, scavenger-type hunts that add points for prizes with a provided list of places to go and people to meet, plus other fun activities. Gamification is another term we use, which really means making it a game to stay engaged and focused on what is happening during the event on the screen.

WELCOME BACK TO PRINCIPLE #8:

*When you have fun and create community,
the memories will follow,
the buzz will follow,
and the money will follow.*

For a conference, I would say the money refers to having more people sign up to attend. Being virtual, they don't need to travel or pay for a hotel room, making it attractive to those who couldn't afford to attend in person.

The memories, the buzz, the money—these are all byproducts of having fun and creating connections. Community is coming together with a unity of purpose. Everyone attending the online event is there for a purpose. Be clear about the purpose, and don't stray from that focus when designing the event.

Taking care of the attendees, the speakers, and the sponsors creates a connection that is reflected in the communications with them via email and sometimes even by phone, as well as how the conference has been organized for them. I always kept in mind the intention that the community is built through this annual conference. We added attendee networking roundtable discussions at the end of the first two days. The topics were culled from those suggested by the attendees. These discussions were very well attended both days, and the time was extended a bit each day as everyone was so engaged in their conversations with lots of sharing among peers. This was a wonderful manifestation of our intention to create ways for the attendees to connect virtually.

To add more networking opportunities, we added two extracurricular activities for other ways attendees could connect and have fun. These were held via Zoom networking sessions. We arranged for a cheese tasting with Point Reyes Farmstead Cheese Company, a local Marin County organic cheesemaker, and a chocolate tasting with Dandelion Chocolate, a local San Francisco company. Attendees were required to place their orders for the cheese and/or chocolates a few weeks prior to the conference, and the product was shipped directly to them before the conference.

At the end of day one, we had a cheese tasting with five cheeses led by a Point Reyes Farmstead Cheese company expert. It was fun to learn about the different award-winning cheeses, how they were made and the difference in tastes. At the end of day two of the conference, we had a chocolate tasting. Dandelion Chocolate works directly with cocoa growers in different countries and their

Point Reyes Farmstead Cheese Company; Dandelion Chocolate

chocolate bars contain just one single origin chocolate and cane sugar. All organic. We were led through tasting the three different chocolate bars. What can be bad about tasting chocolate?! Fun and delicious! Everyone who attended enjoyed these two tastings.

VIRTUALLY TAKING CARE

For the annual in-person conference I have been planning and producing for many years, my staff of twenty-two would arrive for setup the day before the conference begins. Everyone would get started unpacking boxes, getting the registration area ready, putting out signs, setting up the command center, and preparing for the two-day conference. During our lunch break, I would review everyone's assignments—laid out on Excel spreadsheets noting what each person is doing and where they are to be at each moment of time during each conference day. That's their assignment. Then I explain what their real job is—taking care. Taking care of the speakers, the

Everything is an Event 139

sponsors, the attendees, and the committee members. It doesn't matter if the event is a virtual one, there is still the need to be aware of taking care of everyone who is present. This may include handling any questions or concerns that arise via email or assisting with a technology problem during the virtual event.

Being sensitive in planning a virtual conference is the awareness that people are sitting and watching a screen. How do we keep them engaged and enthusiastic about being part of the conference? Surprise is one element or something that shakes things up a bit. During short fifteen-minute breaks, we provided "Get Up and Stretch" sessions with a yoga teacher to lead exercises for ten minutes, allowing for a five-minute pause before the next speaker session. Helping everyone to move around a bit and get their energy moving before the next educational session says we are thinking of you and taking care. These Get Up and Stretch sessions turned out to be very popular with the attendees.

VIRTUAL EVENT DESIGN

The design of a virtual event has the same considerations as an in-person event. The look and feel of the space are important. For a virtual event, this means the design of the graphics for the virtual event platform. The visuals need to be pleasing and easy on the eye as well as have clarity about where to go next and what to do when they arrive. The online virtual event platform we chose provided ease for the attendees to move through the conference day and find all the sessions they wanted to attend.

The platform worked great for the first two days, but on the third day of the conference, the virtual event platform was not working! At 7:30 a.m., our team met in our Zoom green room to check in—the green room was for emergencies primarily. There were five of us—the webmaster, my assistant director, the conference chair, our tech coordinator, and myself. The tech coordinator explained that the platform was not working for the speakers' sessions. She said, "Whatever we do, we must do it now!" We moved into action to pivot and switch all fourteen speaker sessions for the day to Zoom webinars. The opening keynote started forty-five minutes later than scheduled, and while that session was going on, our team was getting all the pieces in order to rebuild the day's sessions. I created a list of the speakers and their committee moderators' emails for our conference chair to send them the new link for their Zoom sessions. I already had a list of all speakers with their emails and cell numbers in case we needed to reach any of them during the conference.

My assistant director was communicating with the committee members, letting them know to tell their speakers new links were being sent for their sessions. Our Sponsor Committee Chair emailed all the sponsors to let them know their sessions would be thirty minutes later than originally scheduled. Our webmaster was taking the Zoom links and putting them in the online platform schedule. Oh, to add to the "fun," our website crashed, and the webmaster had to fix that! Which she did. We moved all the scheduled times thirty minutes later than originally planned—and we still ended up with the closing keynote speaker at the same time. Our tech team was making all the changes needed for all the speaker sessions on the back end. All this during the morning keynote session. Whew!

Our team continued to "hang out" in the Zoom green room as the day progressed. Yes, I was still constantly answering emails, my assistant director was responding to committee communications, our webmaster was monitoring the conference as it continued, and our Tech Coordinator was overseeing the backend technology.

This brings me to an important note about what an event designer's job really is. Yes, planning ahead is a big part of it. By planning ahead and doing the event before the event as I have mentioned before—for the virtual event, it was reviewing the production schedule over and over—everything timed to the minute for each day, we are prepared for what is planned and have anticipated and solved any breakdowns in advance that we could identify. Therefore, we can be present and ready for whatever else may arise in the moment. Which definitely was the case for this virtual conference. **Most importantly, the event designer's job is to create the team.** Creating a team that handles different aspects of the event, and meeting with them often to review the plans means that everyone is on the same page pulling together. Another example of community. Coming together in a unity of purpose.

REMEMBER,
HOW YOU DO ONE THING IS HOW YOU DO EVERYTHING.

The event designer is the orchestrator, following up with each member of the team during the live event. How you do your meetings and reviews with your team shows up in the end result of your event. Because we had reviewed and "done the event before the event" many times while reviewing the production schedule over many team meetings, we were primed to be present to handle whatever showed up in the moment. It did, and we did what needed to be done to remedy the situations that arose. That's what a prepared team does. *The show must go on!*

VIRTUAL, IN PERSON, AND HYBRID

There is a lot of talk about hybrid events. That means an in-person event AND a virtual event happening at the same time. Actually, these are TWO events. The needs of an in-person event are different from a virtual event. I am finding that everyone has a different definition of hybrid. What that says to me is that no one really knows what hybrid is, but it sounds good. "Yes, we are inclusive; we are doing a live in-person and live virtual event." Do you see that there might be a problem here? Two different audiences! Two different expectations. Two different ways of providing information and connecting with people. Remember the principle "what you focus on increases"? Focusing on two simultaneous events is more than a bit challenging. Yes, you can do this if you have a lot of money to handle the technology required to do both at the same time and the staff for two different teams—one handling the live event and one producing the virtual event. If your budget is limited, I suggest you focus on one event at a time. For our conference, we decided to provide a **live virtual** event and then offered on-demand sessions afterward for attendees to view educational sessions and get additional CE credit. Be clear about the purpose of your event as that is the foundation for building a successful event.

There are, of course, advantages to virtual events as anyone can attend no matter where they are located in the world—even those who never could travel to an event can participate virtually. Many events are designed to be only virtual for this very reason. Certainly, the reach of who can be part of the virtual event is greatly expanded. Technology has provided many more options and improvements since the pandemic forced us to be virtual.

A VIRTUAL MEMORIAL

During the time of lockdown, I helped coordinate an online memorial. The purpose was to bring everyone invited together to honor and remember the deceased. We held a practice the day before with two people handling the Zoom technology—to let everyone into the gathering, to show a slide show of photos and play music at the beginning, and to mute or unmute people as they shared their memories. It turned out to be a very moving and meaningful ceremony, modeled after a Quaker meeting. It felt very personal and connected with everyone who was present. In some ways, it was even better, as there were people joining from the East Coast to the West Coast. If it had been held in person, not everyone would have been able to travel for the gathering. In a Quaker meeting, anyone can speak if they feel moved to do so. At the end of the main program, after so many had shared their memories and experiences about the deceased, we were put into groups in breakout rooms that allowed our smaller groups to meet and chat. This provided time for more sharing and connecting. The two hours went by quickly during a very heartfelt time together.

WHEN VIRTUAL IS A FILM

In the summer of 2021, I was asked to plan and coordinate a celebration of life for someone who was a major philanthropist. I had actually worked for her many years ago and had planned and coordinated several events for her and her husband over the years. The plan was to have a celebration at a beautiful location in San Francisco where the family and friends, traveling from across the country, could each take the stage and share something meaningful. Music was also to be included in the program, and afterward, a caterer would serve drinks and pass around hors d'oeuvres. Protocol required that all guests show proof of vaccination and their ID. They were requested to wear a mask for the program and until the refreshments were served in the lobby.

In six weeks, I had planned and confirmed all the elements: the speakers, musicians, and a caterer for the event. I had ordered printed invitations after working with my graphic designer to design the invitation. The graphic designer also created a program for the event, listing all who were speaking and the musicians who would be playing. There were lots of emails, calls, and Zoom meetings with vendors and with the small group leading the vision and making final decisions. Putting this event together required me to create a budget to show all the costs involved, which I reviewed with the finance person who was part of the committee. In early August, with the pandemic still going strong, the committee determined that an in-person event could not happen. We had to cancel what was planned. I sent emails to all the vendors and participants that the in-person event was canceled. The beautifully printed invitations could not be mailed. An email was sent to all the invitees to notify them of the canceled event. Now what?

After much conversation, it was decided to film the family and friends who were going to speak at the in-person event. They were located across the country, from New Hampshire to Hawaii, with others in Northern and Southern California. This event project required a different team. I hired a director and producer to make this happen. I became the project coordinator, which is really another name for event planner. Now, a new budget was required, and approval was made to go ahead with this project.

More emails, Zoom meetings, and phone calls were required with all those who would be filmed. The plan was to get all filmed in the month of September, which required the producer to hire film crews for Hawaii, New Hampshire, San Francisco, and Southern California. This required a lot of coordination to confirm dates with the people speaking and with the film crews. The film crew included a camera person, a lighting person, and a sound tech. With the filming in Hawaii and New Hampshire, the director zoomed in so she could guide the film crew and the person speaking. In San Francisco, there was the camera crew with lighting and sound people, plus a makeup person—and the producer and director on-site. With film, the makeup person doesn't change the person's appearance but just makes them look better in the lighting and for the camera. You would never know they had any makeup done.

The director worked individually with each person speaking prior to filming. Each person had to write out their speech, and the director coached them on their presentation, the spacing, their breathing, pausing, plus what they should wear on camera. Speaking to a camera is very different from speaking to a group from a podium. There are tricks and tips to make the filmed presentation as professional as possible. The director coached each person several times over Zoom to practice their speech and get comfortable being filmed. I created a film outline, which was really a timeline noting the order of who was speaking and for how long and what slides were needed for each "section."

By the end of September, everyone had been filmed—with more work now to be done and so many details to be filled in to make this film ready by the end of October! You can't just have talking heads on a film, so each person speaking chose photos to be shown that correlated with their speech. However, once the producer started putting it all together, it was revealed that there were not enough photos. You can't just have one photo for a minute of talking. So, I started looking for photos, and my graphic designer also researched photos. The graphic designer also created slides that stated each person's name and relationship to the deceased to introduce them before their talk. I found sunset pictures that became the background for each of these slides. Graphics were also needed to frame the opening slide with a beautiful photo of the deceased. With eight speakers, one close friend singing two songs at the beginning and end, plus a musical interlude with two musicians on piano and bass—also filmed—there were so many details, emails, communications, and even more with the producer and director and me to get this project to completion. I have so many folders on my computer filled with all the information and planning that this project required.

We considered whether there needed to be background music while people spoke. This was discussed and music were options explored. Finally, it was decided that music was not needed. There was enough music in the program already. I suggested using Paperless Post to send invitations to all invitees to notify them of the celebration film to be released on a Saturday in late October. Many choices of designs were reviewed, and finally, an invitation design was chosen. I set up the Paperless Post account and added all the invitees—over 200 of them.

But wait, there's more! To show the film, we needed a website. I had my website person create a site, just one page, very simple where the film could be seen starting with the Saturday October date and thereafter. Yes, this was still an event with a date where everyone could watch the film when it was first released on the website. To have a website, we first had to get a domain name, and the site then had to be designed and approved. The setup required lots of technology, which is not my category. However, I knew who to call! The website address was included in the Paperless Post announcement to all the invitees.

This was such a different event than any I had ever done before; however, it was still an event with a specific event date, invited guests, and a committee that helped make all the decisions along the way. Rather than walking into a physical event, the look and feel of this event were expressed through the design of the website, the design of the film, and with the invitations and communications via Paperless Post. The purpose was still a celebration of life for an extraordinary woman.

It was quite a push to finalize all the details to get the film finished and approved by the committee and posted on the website to go live on the October Saturday date. The reward? Many glowing reviews and feedback. One wrote in an email, "The virtual celebration of life was wonderful—beautiful and elegant, just as she would have liked. Compliments to all of you and to the family for a remembrance that was really quite perfect."

When I begin working on an event, my crystal ball does not reveal how the event will unfold. I start with the purpose of the event, which is always the foundation before any planning begins. Just like building a house, you first need a firm foundation. Many times, people forget to do the foundational work before starting to plan.

WHAT ARE THE TOP FIVE THINGS TO REMEMBER FOR A VIRTUAL EVENT?

1. **Build a foundation—clarity of purpose**
2. **Build a team—this includes the client, the committee, and the staff**
3. **Hire competent, professional technical staff**
4. **Create a production schedule that lists all actions and the timing for the virtual event**
5. **Meet with the team consistently and review the plans and production schedule over and over**

"It takes as much energy to wish as it does to plan."

–Eleanor Roosevelt

Chapter Eight
In Conclusion

At this point, you may be thinking you still can't do this. Does it seem like I can do this but you can't? I don't believe it, and it is why I have shared what I know in this book and have taught clients over many years so they can plan and produce their own events. I know you can do this!

I believe that planning and producing events is fun. Start with the why—the **purpose** of your event. That will get you going in the right direction and thinking positively about your party, volunteering for your nonprofit's gala, your daughter's wedding, or even your child's birthday party. Also important is to ask yourself, what is the **experience** you want you and your guests to have? What do you want the **atmosphere** to feel like? Go back and do the **Energy Bubble** exercise (Chapter One page 20) to clarify your intention.

Yes, you have to write everything down. This helps bring your vision into physical manifestation. Plus, order creates greater calm and peace of mind, remember? Use the tools outlined in Chapters Two and Four. Make your binder and folders on your computer. I do this for every event.

Anticipation is a constant activity. At the heart of planning is continuing to anticipate what the event needs to get it to the finish line. Always be looking at the big picture and the micro details. I get excited as all the elements start to come together and I can really visualize what the event will look like and feel like. My energy of excitement is knowing that this event will be wonderful for all the guests, and it will be joyful. Don't we want to spread more joy? Since every event is about creating connection, joy is an attractor, an experience that people do want. When you welcome your guests and appreciate them, you are spreading joy. Remember, what you focus on increases.

So go have fun creating the parties and events you envision. Practice the principles in this book and see how they work for you. It doesn't matter if your event is small or large, and don't forget—whoever shows up are the right people! Be present with all those in attendance. No need to be disappointed as some guests cannot attend.

Life happens and not everyone can join your party. It's too bad they will miss the fun you have created!

How you think about your event will permeate every aspect of it. Use the mantras in Chapter Three to shift your thinking to the positive qualities you want to experience at your event. Think about what you want guests to say when they arrive and what you want them to say when they leave. Hold these visions in mind.

Here's a quote that I have paraphrased to apply to your thinking and to your event:

> Don't speak negatively about yourself or your event even as a joke.
>
> Words are energy and cast spells, that's why it's called spelling.
>
> Change the way you speak about yourself and your event, and you open the door to new possibilities. .
>
> And . . . *you and your guests will experience the wonderful event you envisioned.*

If you find you are planning an event that is larger than you feel you can take on by yourself, get the help you need from a professional caterer or event planner. Or hire staff to assist you if that is what is needed. Each event has different requirements. Remember to always claim EASE in the planning and implementation of your events. I do.

Get out your magic wand—all the power in your wand is explained in this book—and cast spells for your amazing event. Build your Energy Bubble with your purpose and intentions for the experience and atmosphere you desire—and have fun all along the way!

Oh . . . and remember, it's not over when it's over! There's follow-up (yes, before, during, and after), and the big benefit is the fond memories your guests will be talking about for weeks, months, and maybe even years!

Appendices

Appendix A

The 15 Event Principles

1. Clarity of Purpose (page 11)

2. Every Event Is an Experience (page 12)

3. Creating Connection and Community Is the Point of All Events (page 12)

4. Be Aware of the Flow (page 15)

5. Clarity of Intention (page 16)

6. What You Focus on Increases (page 16)

7. When You Place Your Attention on Your Intention—with Clarity of Purpose—You Can Manifest the Desired Result (page 16)

8. When You Have Fun and Create Community, the Memories Will Follow, the Money Will Follow, the Buzz Will Follow (page 17)

9. Build the Atmosphere (page 20)

10. Order Creates Greater Calm and Peace of Mind (page 25)

11. Small Details Can Equal Big Consequences (page 35)

12. How You Think Comes Before You Take Action (page 43)

13. Time Travel—Do the Event Before the Event (page 73)

14. Décor—The Rule of Three (page 95)

15. Take Care of Everyone (page 128)

Appendix B
Event Timelines

....

SUMMER DINNER PARTY EVENT TIMELINE

(SEE PAGE 107 FOR MORE ABOUT THIS)

Tuesday, July 5	Email invitivtation to 9 friends for my August 13th Dinner Patio Party
	Track replies
Monday, July 25	Reserve tables & chairs with Rental Company
Monday, August 1	Buy potting soil and a few plants to dress up the patio, also small potted plants for table
Wednesday, August 3	Clean house and sweep the patio, fluff the plants in pots
Thursday, August 4	Email to guests - reconfirm time of arrival, bring a hat for the sun and a beverage, list menu, ask others to bring hors d'euvres. Susan bringing Deviled Eggs. John & Brooke are bringing salads (green salad, quinoa salad)
Friday, August 5	email to confirm other hors d'oeuvres being brought
Tusday, August 9	Shop Farmer's Market for berries, corn and tomatoes
Wednesday, August 10	Shop grocery store for foods on list
	Cook corn, cut off the cob, refrigerate
Thursday, August 11	Purchase small mum plants, repot in terracotta pots
	Make Sauce Verte and refrigerate
Friday, August 12	
8:30 AM	Make cake frosting & refrigerate
12:00 PM	Bake cake
2:00 PM	Pick up rentals - 2 tables and 6 black folding chairs
4:30 PM	Pick up last few items at grocery store
	Set up tables on Patio - long dining table, buffet and bar
	Make raspberry filling for cake
Saturday, August 13	
8:00 AM	Pick up card tables at Target
9:00 AM	Pedicure appointment
10:00 AM	Assemble and frost cake, refrigerate
11:00 PM	set all tables with underskirt linen and cotton ikat overays. Set dinner table with silver flatware, napkins, plates, glasses and potted mums
2:00 PM	Prep and bake salmon, make corn tomato basil salad & refrigerate
	Set out all serving bowls, platters and serving untencils
4:00 ppm	Pull out of fridge: corn tomato basil salad, Sauce Verte (put in serving bowl); put salmon on platter with curly parsley around it. On Bar: Put bags of ice over drinks in two ice tubs (Hint water and wine/champagne) and in ice bucket
4:30 PM	Dressed and ready for party!
5:00 PM	Guest arrive! Drinks and hors d'oeuvres on the patio
6:00 PM	Dinner buffet set out and served
8:30 - 9:00 pm	Guests depart

ELAINE & LYMAN WEDDING WEEKEND EVENT TIMELINE
(SEE PAGE 123 FOR MORE ABOUT THIS)

Thursday, June 16	
8:30 AM	Marinda to call Lyman and Heidi/Rental Co. re tents or no tents; heaters, etc.
	(Rental Co. xxx-xxx-xxxx) (Lyman xxx-xxxx)
3:00 PM	George/Florist brings house arrangements, arrange florals
	& in garden; potted plants for Rehearsal/Brunch centerpieces &
	5 bathrooms. (O: xxx-xxxx) (cell xxx-xxxx)
	Marinda arrives to meet George/Florist(cell: xxx-xxxx)
3:00 - 5:00 PM	Rental company delivery (tables, chairs, linen) and placed in garage
Friday, June 17	
11:00 am - 8:00 PM	Robert/Lighting Company team on site for lighting set up (cell: xxx-xxx-xxxx)
12:00 - 2:00 PM	George/Florist installs flower border (xxx-xxxx) (c xxx-xxxx)
3:30 PM	Ann & Catering staff arrives (xxx-xxxx)
	Marinda on site (cell: xxx-xxxx)
5:30 PM	Best Western Inn shuttle to leave hotel to client's home
	Hotel Contact, Natalie (xxx-xxxx)
5:30 - 6:00 PM	Guests arrive for Rehearsal and Dinner
	Nametags set out for guests; table names & place cards at tables
6:30 PM	Rehearsal in garden
7:00 PM	Hors d'euvres and drinks served in living room
7:30 PM	Dinner in Famly Room
9:30 PM	Guests depart
	Best Western Inn shuttle takes guests back to hotel
1:30 PM	Ann & Catering staff arrives
	Marinda arrives
2:00 PM	Persia arrives for Bride's hair and makeup
	Florist delivers wedding flowers (xxx-xxxx) (cell xxx-xxxx)
	Marinda's assistant, Esther, arrives (cell xxx-xxxx)
3:30 PM	Ken & Band arrives to set up (Ken C: xxx-xxx-xxxx)
	Jeffery/Photographer arrives (Cell: xxx-xxx-xxxx)

1

Everything is an Event

ELAINE & LYMAN WEDDING WEEKEND EVENT TIMELINE CON'T.

Saturday, June 1	
4:00 PM	Classical trio arrives for ceremony & receiption (Moses: cell xxx-xxxx)
4:00 PM	Valet Parking service staff arrive (xxx-xxxx)
4:15 PM	Shuttle van arrives at Best Western Inn
	(xxx-xxx-xxxx)
	Deborah/Phtographer arrives, sets up for "photo guest book"
4:30 PM	Shuttle van departs Best Western Novato Oaks Inn to 100 Garner
	Guests begin to arrive
	Classical trio playing in garden
5:00 PM	Wedding Ceremony in garden
5:30 PM	Guests follow Elaine & Lyman up the stairs to front of the house
	for cocktails and hors d'oeuvres
	Classical Trio goes up back stairs to front of house
	Photo Guest Book activity w/Deborah
	Catering staff set up dining tables & heaters in garden area
7:00 PM	Bride & Groom follows guests down to dinner in the garden
	Family style service at tables
7:30 - 7:45 PM	First Dance - Elaine & Lyman - After All
	Let the dancing begin! (2 songs chosen by Elaine & Lyman)
9:15 - 9:30 PM	Toasts and cake cutting
	Dessert buffet - with coffee, tea, chocolate dipped strawberries.
9:45 PM	More dancing! (First song: *I knew the Bride when She used to Rock and Roll* !)
11:00 PM	Music over. Guests depart
	Shuttle van takes last group back to Novato Oaks Inn
Sunday, June 19	
9:00 AM	Ann & Catering staff arrive
	Robert and crew breakdown lights
9:30 AM	Marinda arrives
10:00 AM	Robert and crew depart, lighting removed
11:00 AM	Guests arrive
	Brunch Buffet & beverages served
1:00 PM	Brunch over. Guests depart
Monday, June 20	
	Rentals picked up (tables, chairs, linen, etc.)

Everything is an Event

BIG SUR WEDDING LENI & BRYANT EVENT TIMELINE
(SEE PAGE 74 FOR MORE ABOUT THIS)

	Marinda cell: 415-XXX-XXXX
	Qualities: Celebration, Community, Family, Connection, Peace, Harmony, Beauty, Openness, Relaxed, Casual, Elegant, Accessible, Surprise, Fun, Joy, Gratitude, Blessed, Oneness, Humor, Inspiration
Thursday, August 22	
	Leni & Bryant arrive at Ventana Inn.
	Marinda picks up linen at Big 4 Rents and easel at CMS
Friday, August 23	
9:00 - 9:30 am	Marinda departs for Big Sur
1:00 PM	Marinda arrives at Big Sur Lodge
	Marinda on site - bringing linen Friday Dinner, pinatas, nametags, escort cards, placecards, table name cards, goody bags, programs, clothespins, Truffles, straight pins, Kit & Items from Leni - 2 urns, buddha, incense holder, cloth for altar, 2 baskets for flower girls, blindfold
2:00 PM	Lucia Room Set up for Dinner Party - Marinda review with Michael Z, F&B Manager
	Kate, Florist delivers zinnia centerpieces (Ce;; XXX-XXXX) return vases at Ventana?
	Sound system set up with microphone & speakers, ipod plugged in for music (get iPod from Bryant)
4:00 PM	**Rehearsal on Lower Terrrace at Ventana Inn** - Leni, Bryant, Marilyn, Tucker, Giovanna, Rick, Abby, Paul, Cate, Ella, Sophie, & Marinda (Marinda gets White Tara Thangka from Giovanna)
5:00 PM	Marinda back at Lucia Room, Big Sur Lodge
5:45 PM	Leni and Bryant arrive at Lucia Room & Patio, Big Sur Lodge
6:00 PM	**Dinner Party Begins!**
	Guests arrive and are welcomed! Receive nametags and table take-in cards to find their places at the tables. Marinda tells them there is a gift to pick up when they leave. (ask guests to please take photos and post on website)
	Glasses of wine and mineral water passed. Tables with fruits & cheeses, and salsas and chips. Bar with bartender.
7:00 - 7:15 PM	Guests invited to be seated at their tables
7:00 - 7:15 PM	Leni and Bryant welcome & introduce their guests (wireless mike) - give Leni & Bryant lists
7:30 PM	Guests invited to the dinner buffet
	Marinda hangs pinatas for the girls to swing at (with blindfold)
8:30 PM	Dessert served, coffee and tea served
8:30 PM	Bryant invites guests to toast Leni & Bryant (idenitified beforehand)
9:00 -9:30 PM	Bryant thanks guests for being here and reminds them to pick up their gift bags at the recepction table as they leave. Marinda will hand them out. Lisa to help give flowers to guests, vases saved for florist.
8:00-11:30 am	Breakfast on your own at Big Sur Lodge served from 8:00 - 11:30 am.
10:00 AM	**Bryant with family and friends - Off on a hike.** Gather in lobby at Big Sur Lodge.

Everything is an Event

BIG SUR WEDDING LENI & BRYANT EVENT TIMELINE CON'T.

Saturday, August 24	
2:00 PM	Marinda on site at Ventana Lower Terrace to meet Kate, DJ, Musicians, set up of ceremony and altar
	DJ Daryl L. (Cell XXX-XXXX) arrives to set up sound for ceremony, then set up for reception.
2:30 PM	Wedding flowers delivered by Kate to Ventana Inn. Deliver Bridal flowers to Leni's room.
3:00 PM	Wedding Ceremony set up on Lower Terrace - 2 urns with flowers, 6-footx18" table for altar: altar cloths, candles/hurricanes, urns, buddha, incense burner, 2 armless chairs for musicians, reserved signs /ribbons for family members in first rows, easel for White Tara Thangka
	Earlier wedding reception concludes on Upper Terrace
3:30 PM	Musicians arrive - harp & flute - Diana S. (cell:XXX-XXXX) & Shawna S. check in with Marinda - get plugged in by DJ Daryl
4:00 PM	Reception tables set up on Upper Terrace for Reception; Gifts & guest cards table set up, table name signs, placecards and escort cards set up, places for large arrangments, heaters
	Videographer, Dakota B. (cell: XXX-XXXX) on site for set up
4:15 PM	Gary F., Photographer, photographs Leni & bridal party in her room
4:20 PM	Bryant, Marilyn, Tucker, Giovanna & Rick gather to get wedding corsages and boutonnieres pinned on
4:30 PM	Musicians begin to play for ceremony
	Guests begin to arrive
4:30 PM	Gary, Photographer back
5:00 PM	**Wedding Ceremony begins**
	Processional: Butterfly Jump Like a Rabbit - Giovanna & Rick, Orgyen Chowang Rinpoche, Bryant & Marilyn, Tucker
	Wedding Processional: Chanters Tune - Cate, Ella, Sophie, Abby and Leni
5:30 PM	Ceremony concludes
	Recessional: Rinpoche, Leni & Bryant, Giovanna & Rick, Abby & Tucker, Cate, Ella, Sophie & Paul, Marilyn & Scott and guests to Upper Terrace.
	Wedding Reception begins
	Waiters greet guests with trays of wine and mineral water. Hors d'oeuvres passed
	Table with escort cards - Marinda to greet, invite guests to take their card
	Diana & Shawna move to Upper Terrace to play harps, flute
	Large arrangements move to reception, altar flowers go to bridal table - Joni & team
6:00 PM	Family group photos. Lisa to assist in gathering family members. Plus portraits of Leni & Bryant.
	Marinda breakdowns altar and packs up items, Candles & hurricanes go to Kate, the florist
6:30 PM	Photos complete. Leni & Bryant back with their guests
7:15 PM	Guests invited to be seated at their tables - first course salad plated
	Jerry and Diane give a blessing (wireless mike)
	DJ Daryl plays background music. Diana & Shawna depart.

158 *Everything is an Event*

BIG SUR WEDDING LENI & BRYANT EVENT TIMELINE CON'T.

Saturday, August 24	
7:45 PM	First Dance - Leni and Bryant
7:50 PM	Guests invited to join Leni and Bryant on the dance floor - Dance Set
7:53 PM	Sunset (sunrise 6:33 am)
8:05 PM	Guests invited to the dinner buffet - plates served to Leni, Bryant & Rinpoche
8:30-8:40 PM	Dance Set
8:55 PM	Champagne passed on trays to guests for toast
9:00 PM	Cake cutting and Toasts - Harry/Dad, Abby, Tucker, Marilyn (wireless mike)
9:25 PM	Dance Set
10:00 PM	DJ stops playing - or continues for 1/2 hour? Guests depart - or not!
10:00 PM	Videographer departs. Photographer departs
10:30 PM	Amplified music ends - per Ventana
	Large arrangements to The Gallery for breakfast gathering Sunday am. Centerpiece flowers distributed to guests, vases back to Kate/Florist
Sunday, August 25	
9:30 AM	**Breakfast Gathering at Ventana Inn in The Gallery.** Guests to go to main buffet in Restaurant
10:30 AM	Breakfast buffet closes
12:00 PM	Guests depart - or not!
	Marinda departs for San Francisco
Monday, August 26	
AM	Marinda delivers to vendors the rental linens and easel

Everything is an Event 159

BLANK EXCEL EVENT TIMELINE

Day, Date, Year	
	Add qualities of your event here from the Energy Bubble
Time	Action to be taken, or contact with Cell # and action
Time	
Time	
Time	
Time	
Time	
Time	
Time	
Day, Date, Year	Each page should have this day, date, year at the top
Time	
Time	
Time	
Format your document.	
Set your alignment to Top - easier to see the times & actions listed	
I use the lines on the screen but I print the timeline without the gridlines.	
It's cleaner and easier to read.	
With Page Set up - in Margins, center the document, Add Header (title of timeline and event date) and add Footer for page numbers and date	

Appendix C
Diagrams

Here's a way to visualize the order you create to produce your event. The EVENT is at the center. All the aspects surrounding serve the center — the EVENT. They are essential to your success. The Mantras are your thoughts and how you think about what you envision (see Chapter Three, page 43). The Flow is explained on page 15. Chapters Two and Four explain the tools required for order and ease of planning and production. Review Chapter One again for the Purpose for your event and Atmosphere you design — both important!

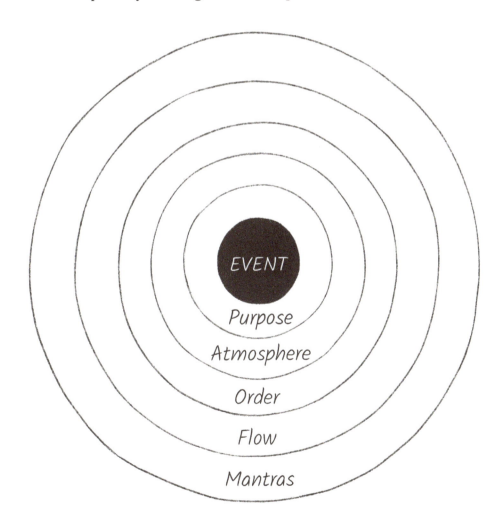

Everything is an Event 161

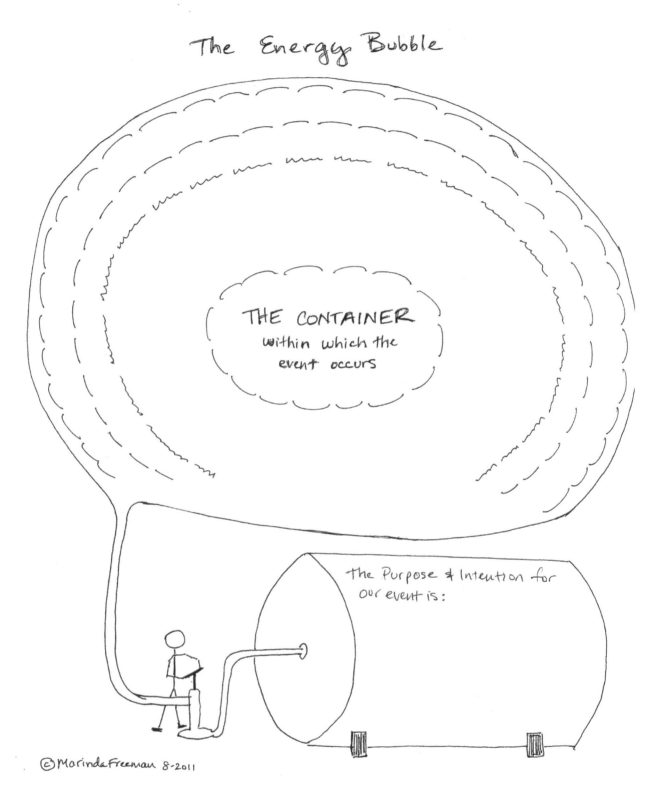

Here's the Energy Bubble for you to fill out. Make copies and write your clear purpose and intention for your event in the tank. Fill in the Bubble with the qualities you want your guests to experience.

Appendix D

Prepping for Thanksgiving and any Holiday Meal

PREPPING FOR THANKSGIVING . . . WITH EASE

Are you daunted by the looming Thanksgiving holiday dinner? How to get everything ready for the family and friends who will be descending on Thursday? Is it possible to be relaxed in your planning and preparation? Can you really enjoy the day? Yes! Try following these steps and suggestions and see if you can ease up on the stress and have more fun.

Note: the planning outlined here can also apply to any holiday dinner party you want to host.

1. Write out your menu at least a couple weeks ahead of Thanksgiving. Determine what you will be making and what you will ask others to bring.

2. Designing the menu.
   - For me, this means listing the non-negotiable items first — turkey, stuffing, cranberry sauce, sweet potatoes and/or mashed potatoes. Since everything is white or orange with a dash of cranberry, green is needed.
   - That means vegetables — at least two dishes. Be creative. Yes, you can do basic green beans, but why not do something a little different? It's also helpful to make one or both dishes that can be made earlier in the day and served at room temperature. See below some vegetable suggestions.

3. Plan what you will make on what days. Some suggestions for timing are:
   - Cooked cranberry sauce can be made days ahead. Raw cranberry orange relish can be made the day before.
   - Shopping for most ingredients can be done five days to a week ahead.
   - Purchase your turkey a week ahead so it can defrost in the refrigerator. If you get a fresh turkey, of course, there's no defrosting. I like the dry brine recipes — easier to do than immersing the turkey in liquid. Who has the space for that?!

Everything is an Event

- Pies – the pie dough can be made days ahead and refrigerated. Pies can be made the day before.
- Vegetables – Thanksgiving day while the turkey is roasting.
- Mashed potatoes and/or sweet potatoes — the day of.
- Gravy – after the turkey is out of the oven and you can access the drippings. I use cornstarch instead of flour to thicken the gravy — which takes care of anyone that's gluten-free. No one has ever noticed it's not flour in all the years I've made it this way.

4. What to ask others to bring? Call them up to ask what they are thinking of bringing or, conversely, give them one or two suggestions from your list of what you would like them to bring. See below for vegetable side dish suggestions. Let them know how many will be coming for dinner. Confirm the prepared dish they will bring (emphasize prepared — you don't want them making it at your house). Be clear about what time they should plan to arrive.

5. Set the table the day before Thanksgiving or the day before that. Use linen tablecloth and napkins, low centerpiece (no higher than twelve inches) of flowers or harvest gourds, and small pumpkins plus votive candles or tapers. I get inspired setting a beautiful table — anticipating family and friends coming together. I believe that if the table is attractively and elegantly set, I don't have to get dressed up.

6. After setting the table, pull out all the serving dishes and put Post-it notes in each one naming the dish it will hold. Put the required serving utensils in each serving dish.

7. Set aside the dessert plates and forks/spoons so they are ready with your pies and serving utensils - —knives and pie servers.

8. Take the two-minute guest exercise (Page 14). Start outside your front door, walk in and look around your home to see if there is anything that needs to go away. You can move those items or you can drape them in fabric or sheets to make then disappear. Do you need to open up the space for all the guests gathering? Will you set up some hors d'oeuvres on the coffee table or another place that guests will first gather? Have you set up a bar with beverages and glasses, so guests can help themselves? The goal is to create a relaxed and welcoming atmosphere.

9. Remember that this day is set aside for gratitude and thanksgiving. By planning ahead, you can enjoy the preparation — the cooking and baking — and the celebrating with family and friends. It's good to stop and be grateful for our life, love and connections — and the beauty that surrounds us.

VEGETABLE RECIPE SUGGESTIONS

- Haricots Verts - these French green beans are smaller and cook more quickly. Try them as a salad — blanch and chill, then toss with a balsamic shallot vinaigrette (see recipe on page 166). Serve at room temperature.

- What about brussels sprouts? I've collected a few recipes over the years — roasted with shallots or thinly sliced and sautéed with bacon and served at room temperature. I also love the recipe from Ottolenghi's cookbook, *Plenty More*, with haricots verts, snow peas and broccolini with cilantro in a tahini dressing (the name doesn't do it justice: Sprouting Broccoli with Sweet Tahini, page 69). I've made this a number of times.

- Every year, I make a Butternut Squash Parsnip Puree — that is a requirement by my brother. It's two recipes in one — leftovers can be made into soup. (See recipe on page 167)

- A wonderful recipe for Roasted Parsnips and Sweet Potatoes with Caper Vinaigrette is in Ottolenghi's cookbook, *Plenty*, page 16.

- Carrots sautéed with radicchio - French-cut the carrots and blanch them, then sauté in extra virgin olive oil (EVOO). Toss in thinly sliced radicchio and sauté for a couple minutes. Add salt and pepper, and finish with a few tablespoons of balsamic vinegar. Delicious and great color!

- Another favorite cookbook is *Tartine Every Day* by Elizabeth Prueitt. I'm eyeing her Roasted Fall Vegetables and Apples to make (page 175) in Elizabeth's cookbook.

- Finally, *the New York Times* has many suggestions of what to make and bring when you are the guest. You could suggest a recipe for one of your guests or make one yourself. They sound really delicious.

Everything is an Event

HARICOT VERT SALAD WITH BALSAMIC SHALLOT VINAIGRETTE

I have been making this salad for years. It's a crowd favorite and one of my daughter's favorite recipes.

12-16 oz Haricot Vert (thin green beans)
1/4 cup finely chopped shallots (or a little less, depends on the size of the shallot)
1/2 cup extra virgin olive oil
2-1/2 to 3 Tbsps. balsamic vinegar
2 tsps. Diamond Crystal Kosher Salt
1/8 tsp. ground pepper

Bring a large pot of water to boil. Add the haricot vert and blanch in boiling water for 4 to 5 minutes. Test to make sure cooked but still a little crunchy, not mushy.

Drain into colander and run cold water over beans to stop cooking.

When cooled, line them up in a row along the middle of a towel, fold both long sides over beans and roll up. Chill in refrigerator for at least an hour. This also helps to dry them.

In small mixing bowl or a 1 cup glass Pyrex measuring cup add the finely chopped shallots, the extra virgin olive oil and the balsamic vinegar, salt and pepper.

Whisk together, it should get a little thick. If it's not getting thick, add a little more balsamic.

Let the vinaigrette sit while the beans are chilling. The balsamic vinegar mellows the shallots.

To serve, toss beans in bowl with vinaigrette. Enjoy!

This is even better the next day after the beans have marinated in the dressing in the fridge.

BUTTERNUT SQUASH PARSNIP PUREE

I created this recipe many years ago when my daughter was just starting to eat solid food. It was something everyone could eat at Thanksgiving and Christmas dinner. It's now a required basic on the menu (requested by the men, I might add) for both Thanksgiving and Christmas family meals every year! I always double this recipe, so I have plenty left over to make soup. I've shared this recipe with so many friends and family, and I'm thrilled to share it with you!

- 1 medium/large butternut squash
- 3-4 medium-size parsnips
- 1 stick of butter (cut in slices)
- salt & pepper to taste

Place whole squash on cookie sheet and bake at 350 degrees for one hour. (If it's a large squash, it may need an additional fifteen to thirty minutes more. Cool. Peel. Scrape out seeds and cut into chunks. (Note: sometimes I cook the squash the day before, and once it's cooled, just stick it in the fridge. When I'm ready to make the puree, I will peel it, etc. and then put the chunks in a glass bowl and zap it in the microwave for two to three minutes until it's warm.)

Peel and cut up parsnips into equal size chunks. Place in pot, cover with water, and simmer until soft. Drain.

In food processor, put half of warm squash and parsnips in with half the butter, ½ tsp. salt and ¼ tsp. freshly ground pepper. Puree in food processor, adjust seasonings. (With double the recipe, there will be more batches to put into the food processor.)

And then it's... BUTTERNUT SQUASH PARSNIP SOUP

Put leftover butternut squash parsnip puree in stock pot. Add an equal amount of chicken stock or vegetable stock. Bring to a low simmer. If soup is still too thick, add some more chicken/vegetable stock. Adjust seasonings — salt and pepper. Serve with a garnish of fresh chives. (Cut chives with scissors over each bowl — or mug — of soup just before serving.) This is also a wonderful wintry hors d'oeuvre served in cups or mugs.

Everything is an Event

Appendix E

Hors d'oeuvre Menu Suggestions

I've been designing menus for clients for forty years. I always think about what is most appropriate for the occasion and aligned with what my client wants. My proposals always included options for the client to choose from. For cocktail receptions for hundreds of guests, the menu would include four warm and four cold passed hors d'oeuvres and something on the bars for guests to help themselves.

HORS D'OEUVRES (remember, these are **bite-size savories** and not messy)

I planned and coordinated the cocktail receptions at Sotheby's in New York for eight years. There were many different receptions. Some were for nonprofit organizations. Most were the openings of exhibitions before auctions such as contemporary art, Old Masters, Latin American art, to rare books and manuscripts, Americana furniture, and baseball memorabilia. My most favorite were the Impressionist paintings with walls filled with paintings by Manet, Renoir, Degas, Fantin-Latour, and many others hanging side by side and stacked three high.

There could be as many as five receptions in a month with a range of serving 250 to 400 guests. Some were lunches or dinners for smaller groups. Most were cocktail receptions, which were for two hours. Finger foods that were passed around on silver trays by waiters to the guests. You don't need silver trays, but arranging your hors d'oeuvres on trays makes it easy for guests to help themselves. Always have cocktail napkins to offer when passing hors d'oeurves. Here are some suggestions to consider. Depending on the size of your party, serving at least three different hors d'oeuvres provides some variety. Always consider all diets to make sure you have choices for your guests. Remember to design your menu according to the season. These listed below are from all seasons.

Are you hosting a cocktail party, or a dinner party? If you are hosting a cocktail party, provide eight different hors d'oeuvres. If you are serving hors d'oeuvres before your dinner guests sit down, choose three to four. For either party, think about what can be prepared in advance and already set on a platter in the fridge. Identify warm or room temperature items that are easy to prepare and serve. You want to enjoy your own party, right?!

SERVED WARM:

- Marinated Chicken on Skewers with Mustard Dipping Sauce or Mango Chutney Dipping Sauce
- Baby New Potatoes with Sour Cream & Red Caviar, with Sour Cream and Chives, or with Gruyere & Bacon
- Zucchini Pancakes with Applesauce
- Miniature Tartlets with Brie and Fresh Herbs
- Black Bean Chile in Corn Cups
- Mushrooms Stuffed with Crabmeat or Chopped Spinach & Sage Breadcrumbs
- Crabcakes with Lemon Tartar Sauce
- Wild Mushroom Duxelles in Toast Cups
- Potato Pancakes with Sour Cream and Red Caviar
- Wild Rice Pancakes with Red Pepper Jelly
- Vegetable Fritters with Fresh Ginger
- Skewered Broiled Lamb with Mint Dipping Sauce

SERVED COLD OR AT ROOM TEMPERATURE:

- Filet of Beef on French Bread with Red Pepper Jelly, Horseradish Sauce, or Onion Jam
- Country Pate on Whole Grain Bread with Cornichon
- Ham on Country Bread with Grainy Mustard
- Cucumber Cups with Crab or Shrimp Salad and Fresh Dill or Chicken Salad
- Cognac Chicken Liver Pate on Apple Slices
- Asparagus Wrapped with Prosciutto
- Endive Spears with Herb Cheese or Smoked Salmon Tartare with Lemon & Capers
- Whole Shrimp with Cocktail Sauce
- Curried Egg Salad on Cucumber Rounds or Endive Spears
- Prosciutto-wrapped melon

Everything is an Event

- Smoked Mozzarella and Sun-dried Tomato on Toast Points
- Creamy Sharp Cheddar Spread on Hazelnut Biscuits
- Smoked Trout Spread on Black Bread with Apple Horseradish Sauce
- Pesto Chicken Salad on Whole Grain Bread
- Roast Turkey on Cranberry Bread with Chutney
- Smoked Salmon Mousse on Cucumber Rounds
- Tortellini on Skewers with Pesto Dipping Sauce
- Cherry Tomatoes stuffed with Pesto Chicken Salad
- Cream Cheese and Chutney on Whole Grain Bread
- Tortilla Cups with Guacamole

PLACE ON A TABLE OR ON YOUR BAR:

- Carrot Sticks and String Beans with Boursin Herb Cheese Dip or Artichoke Parmesan Dip
- Asparagus Spears and Endive Leaves with Roasted Red Pepper Dip
- Jicama Sticks and Snow Peas with Fresh Herb Dip
- Carrot Sticks, Parsnips, and Red Pepper Strips with Lemon Zest Dip
- Crock of Creamy Cheeses with Sesame Bread Sticks and French Bread Slices
- Cheddar Cayenne Coins (crackers)
- Guacamole with Tortilla Chips
- Spiced Nuts
- Virginia Peanuts
- Puff Pastry Cheese Straws
- Small bags of Popcorn

There are lots more ideas than these listed, which you can research in wonderful cookbooks and online. This is just to give you some ideas.

Acknowledgments

I could not have written this book without all the wonderful clients I have been blessed to work with over so many years. There are too many to mention, but they know who they are. They have inspired me and allowed me to dig deep into why events work and what is required to make them successful.

Big thanks go to my teacher, Leslie Keenan, whose classes at our wonderful local bookstore, Book Passage, started me on the process of writing what I have learned and taught. She invited me to join her ongoing classes which I have been part of for ten years. My writing group has been a huge support and provided important feedback to my book, so much gratitude to Christine Mann, Madeline Mendelson, Veronica Smith, Marilee Stark, and Anne Ysunza.

I must thank my daughter, Esther, who very kindly allowed me to do my event work and be her mom. My brother, Hunter, and his wife, Leslie, have been awesome cheerleaders for my work. A special salute to Kitty Ault, for the partnership we formed years ago to plan and produce many amazing events for nonprofits and corporations. So many close friends, colleagues and assistants have supported and encouraged me as well as stepped into help with events. I couldn't have done it without them! Kudos to Brooke Beazley, Marian Bradley, Liz Chiarolla, Hannah Dakin, Kim Erixon, Esther Follett, Sami Graf, Betsy Gordon, Jody Heckinlively, Karen Lynch, Nancy Morris, Lesa Porche, Marie Rios, Karaline Stamper, Morgan Smith, Sherry Wickwire, and my Networking Entrepreneurial Women of Marin colleagues. I must also acknowledge my indebtedness to the talented Anne Doyle who designed printed materials for so many of my events and from whom I learned so much.

About the Author

Marinda Freeman is a seasoned event designer renowned for creating experiences that foster connection, comfort, and inspiration. With forty years of expertise, Marinda has planned and produced a variety of events, large and small. Drawing on her experience as a licensed spiritual counselor and teacher, she takes a mindful approach to her work, uniquely blending spirituality and design to enrich her events with a profound sense of purpose and connection.

Marinda is excited to bring what she knows about event planning (and has been teaching clients for many years) to help readers create the events of their dreams with *Everything Is an Event*.

"Everyone always asks me what's my favorite event," Marinda says. "It's always the one I am currently working on. I love the many different kinds of events I have planned and produced, discovering along the way that there are principles that remain the same no matter what kind of event."

Beyond her professional achievements, Marinda is a passionate home chef who has shared her culinary skills through cooking classes for decades. She uses social media to showcase her design work, parties, and culinary creations, reflecting her multifaceted talents and dedication to her craft. You can find her on social media:

 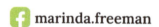 

Reach out to Marinda –
she'd love to hear from you!

marindafreeman.com
everythingisanevent.net

www.ingramcontent.com/pod-product-compliance
Ingram Content Group UK Ltd.
Pitfield, Milton Keynes, MK11 3LW, UK
UKHW050741030225
454604UK00015B/142